Moses
Minim

C000097270

Form Criticism vs. Fiction in the Pentateuch

Robert M. Price

Tellectual Press

tellectual.com

Tellectual
Press

Tellectual Press

tellectual.com
Valley, WA

Print ISBN: 978-1-942897-01-9

Tellectual Press is an imprint of Tellectual LLC.

Table of Contents

This book is for my friend
and partner in Bible Geekery,
JOHN FELIX

Introduction

The Myth of Moses

Having written many (maybe too many!) books on the Christ Myth Theory, I have taken to suggesting that the whole idea might better be dubbed "New Testament Minimalism." As with the once-fringe but now widely influential school of criticism called Old Testament Minimalism, it dares to proclaim that its very subject of study might be lacking in historical substance. Scholars of the Hebrew Bible—including Marc Zvi Brettler, Thomas L. Thompson, Niels Peter Lemche, Philip R. Davies, and Giovanni Garbini—have demonstrated that the utter lack of archaeological support for the traditional picture of Israelite origins implies a much more mundane, much less spectacular "historical Israel" and that by far most of the Old Testament narrative is sheer fiction.

Thus the superstar of the *Old* Testament finds himself subject to the same wilting hot light of historical inquiry that I have tried to shine on the *New*, along with the likes of Richard Carrier, Earl Doherty, Raphael Lataster, D.M. Murdock, René Salm, and Frank Zindler. As with Jesus, there is no tracing the growth rings of the Mosaic oak to get back to a historical Moses acorn, no historical starting point for the process that wound its long way through rabbinical tradition to modern novels and movies.

Those who have witnessed the scorn that is heaped on proponents of the Christ Myth Theory would not be surprised if conservative Jews and Christians found threatening a minimalistic approach to Moses. But Minimalism poses very nearly as great a danger to the work of older generations of scholars including Abraham Kuenen, Julius Wellhausen, Hermann Gunkel, and Martin Noth. Much of the once-regnant source and form criticism is now being ignored or discarded.

Yet, for all my skepticism about the existence of the hero of either Testament, I think this is premature. There was no Moses, but even fiction does not materialize out of thin air. Where did it come from? These older tools of the Higher Criticism can help us answer that question.

———

The Pentateuch (the "Five Books" of Genesis, Exodus, Leviticus, Numbers, and Deuteronomy) gives us the canonical story of Moses. But one must wonder if most Americans get their "information" about this great figure from those texts (well, not counting Genesis, which recounts the time before Moses) or from the cinematic epic *The Ten Commandments* by

Cecil B. De Mille. Of course, the movie takes its inspiration from the Bible (as witness its sometimes fudged pseudo-biblical voice-over), but it also incorporates material from first- century Jewish writers Flavius Josephus and Philo Judaeus, both of whom wrote almost gospel-like accounts of Moses, from his nativity to his assumption into heaven. Not only that, but the script writers added material from no less than three modern Moses novels.[1]

If this saga of Charlton Heston as Moses has loomed larger than Exodus in the popular mind and memory, I view it as quite appropriate. I would argue that in *The Ten Commandments* we have the definitive version of the story, transcending its various source materials, just as it is the James Whale/Boris Karloff *Frankenstein* and the Judy Garland *Wizard of Oz* which are the definitive versions, not the original novels. Thus, any scripture purists griping about artistic license and gratuitous departures from the biblical texts in The Ten Commandments are failing to grasp that the saga of Moses the Lawgiver is a mighty oak, having grown strong and thick through the centuries, with the Pentateuchal version(s) serving as the acorn.

But we can and must go farther: Even the biblical Moses is already a mighty rock with many layers of sediment. Some unnamed, undated compiler wove together four distinct Moses stories, all of them so widely esteemed, each with its own avid partisans, that little or nothing might be omitted. Of these, the most ancient (though perhaps younger than Old Testament critics used to think) was the so-called **J** source, so named for its preferred use of Yahweh (Yahve or Jehovah) for the divine name, and because of its concentration on locales in Judah, the south of the Holy Land.

J was already a Brothers Grimm-like compilation of sacred traditions gathered from campfires and hearths on holy days, or else from shrines, sacred groves, and saints' graves from attendant priests and oracles, each with a kind of "Moses slept here" tale to establish the importance of the place as a pious tourist site. The apparently late **E** source, preferring Elohim for God's name and set in Israel or Ephraim, was a parallel collection from up north.

While both are predominantly narrative, each features greater or lesser portions of Israelite law codes. The **D** source (the Book of Deuteronomy), a century or two later, is almost entirely a subsequent code intended to supplant and update these earlier stipulations. There is a historical prologue concerning Moses and his wandering people, but this is a précis based on the J and E versions, which someone had already combined.

We find the same basic structure in the **P** source, the Priestly Code. There is a historical prologue here, too, but it starts with the seven-day creation, which it recounts in some detail, as it does the Flood of Noah (interspersed by much later editors with a parallel Flood story from J).

Besides this, the rest of the narrative leading up to Moses is the sketchiest of summaries. Once we get to Moses, detail returns, for Moses is the real focus of interest. Most of what is told of him is not told for his sake, but for that of the Torah, the Jewish law, which as we will see is in effect the secret identity of Moses. He is the human face of a personified Torah and little if anything else. This fact becomes apparent when we notice how very many of the Moses episodes are told as *hadith* (to borrow the Islamic, Arabic term) to legitimatize this or that point of Torah by claiming the unassailable authority of Moses on its behalf.

———

Let's jump ahead some centuries to the great Rabbi Judah the Prince in the second century CE (135-219). From at least the establishment of the Yavneh (Javneh, Jamnia) Sanhedrin following the Roman destruction of Jerusalem in 70 CE, the leading rabbis would gather to iron out the proper interpretation and application of the typically quite terse commandments of the Torah. If they were the very orders of God, there was no room for laxity in practice. Granted, the faithful Jew must not work on the Sabbath; that much was clear. But what did and did not count as work? Any physical effort? Or just one's job?

The massive corpus of interpretation and commentary, memorized by rabbis generation after generation, was called the oral tradition. Eventually, Rabbi Akiba was instrumental in systemizing this material, causing it to be collected and written down, a process brought to completion by Judah the Prince. It was called the Mishnah ("the repetition"). A second, auxiliary collection of such traditional legal materials was called the Tosefta ("supplements"). But new questions arose as their successors made the Mishnah the basis of their deliberations, and this material was eventually collected, too, as the Gemara ("study" or "learning").

All these layers of commentary and extrapolation together were codified as the Talmud. There were two independent Talmudic collections, made in two centers of rabbinic learning: the Jerusalem (or Palestinian) Talmud, complied about 435 CE, and the much longer Babylonian Talmud, compiled about 600 CE. ("Talmud" means the same thing as *Gemara*.)

Until Judah the Prince, the tradition of the elders was simply understood along the lines I have suggested. It was authoritative because it was considered the "unpacking" of the divine commandments. But Judah introduced the idea of the oral Torah in the sense that all the Mishnaic material had literally come down from Moses, and in turn from the mouth of God. He had, for some reason, not commanded Moses to write it down, but rather to transmit it orally to the seventy elders called "the Great Assembly" (or "Great Synagogue"), who would transmit it to all subsequent generations.

Obviously this was metaphorical, a pious fiction. You will hardly be surprised when I remind you of the parallels with Jesus and the gospel tradition on the one hand, and the hadith of Muhammad on the other. (To go farther afield, we could add the Buddha.) In those cases, too, massive amounts of teaching and illustrative stories have been collected and grandfathered onto the figurehead prophet. Form criticism, drawing from the individual units of tradition inferences as to where, when, and why they originated, has largely dissolved any historical Jesus into a pile of fragments ("a field of ruins" as Emil Brunner called the gospels).

We cannot really discern whether some historical figure gave rise to the stories and sayings, whether by memory or fabrication, or if Jesus is an artificial magnet around which disparate iron filings congealed. The same is true for Muhammad. Traditionally, the claim was that Muhammad's followers and heirs collected notes and transcriptions of his revelation discourses, and that one or another Caliph had them compiled into the Koran (Qur'an). Now it has become evident that the Koran is simply an earlier collection of (equally inauthentic) hadith, traditions fabricated to advocate various practices and pieties. And once we see that nothing of it goes back to Muhammad, we have to take seriously that he was invented for the purpose. There was no Muhammad. He was the fictive human face of Islamic tradition.

And I'm afraid the same is true for Moses the Lawgiver. He is less historical than Charlton Heston.

————

Drawing on the splendid pioneering work of Hermann Gunkel (1862-1932), father of form criticism, and Martin Noth (1902, 1968), whom one might consider the Old Testament's Rudolf Bultmann, I will scrutinize each and every Moses story, showing how virtually every one was told, actually created, for purposes other than telling us about Moses' life. I will not deal with most of the commandments *per se*. It is easy to show how these laws cannot go back to the ostensible time of Moses (either the 13th or 15th century BCE), as they presuppose a later, settled agricultural way of life.

Not only that, but even a glance at the complexities of Torah tort law makes it obvious we are dealing with almost-rabbinical hair-splitting and nuance that would have been flatly impossible for a bunch of sand-blasted Bedouins. The minutiae of ritual observance on display in the mind-numbing pages of Leviticus simply cannot have governed the rude cult of desert nomads. They are much later stipulations, here projected backwards into the sacred time of origins.

Imagine Moses in the howling wilderness troubling himself or his people about whether to make the Tabernacle draperies out of manatee or dugong hide! So much for the "Mosaic" laws. But we will soon see how even the Moses stories are legal precedents, warrants, and examples. We can follow the fiction created by Judah the Prince all the way back. In other words, Moses *is* the Torah, all the way down.

Gunkel delineated five major categories of biblical myth, differentiated according to what question the ancients were seeking to answer in a pre-scientific, yet ingenious and inventive way. I will add a sixth and outline them here, then group our Moses stories accordingly. The first (in random order) is *Etiological myths*: These are narrative attempts to explain why remarkable things are the way they are, how they came about. Why is there death? Why do we wear clothes? Why must we work for a living? Why do people hate snakes? What is the rainbow? Why do spiders spin webs? [2]

Second come *Etymological myths*: stories explaining, by means of puns, the supposed origins of names no one understood anymore or that had unsavory pagan origins and needed a more wholesome Hebrew explanation. [3]

Third, there are *Ethnological stories*, which depict the relations of nations, tribes, groups in the narrator's day, symbolizing each group as a fictive ancestor who has the stereotype traits of the group. Why do the Israelites and the Edomites always fight, despite being neighbors and even kin? Because Esau and Jacob got off to a bad start, and now it's in the blood. [4]

The fourth are *Geological myths*, folktales told to explain the origin of remarkable features of the landscape, whether oases, springs, wind-eroded rock formations, man-made cairns, glacial megaliths, etc. [5]

Fifth are *Ceremonial myths*, [6] stories told to supply a rationale for performing some ritual or custom that was either so archaic that no one remembered why it was first done, or else pagan in origin and thus requiring a new "orthodox" rationale. These myths are examples of what anthropologist Branislaw Malinowski called *Legitimization myths*: In order to reinforce a society's laws and customs, a story tells that at the dawn of creation God or the gods decreed that it be this way. Who are we to change it now? Of course, the story is told after human beings have created the custom, not before.

I should like to nominate a sixth category, *Cautionary tales*, or *Priestcraft myths*, whose goal is to scare the pious by appeal to fictive examples of ill- fated transgressors of the past. As the old Army VD films used to say, "Men, don't let *this* happen to *you!*"

We will find that a number of our stories fall into more than one of these categories, doing double or triple duty to answer many questions. The stories grew in the telling, as each telling prompted new questions from the audience.[7] New elements were also added during the scribal copying process.[8]

Notes

1. Dorothy Clarke Williams, *The Prince of Egypt* (Philadelphia: Westminster Press, 1949); Joseph Holt Ingraham, *The Pillar of Fire,* or *Israel in Bondage* (NY: A.L. Burt Company, 1859); Arthur E. Southon, *On Eagle's Wing* (NY: McGraw-Hill, 1954).

2. Herman Gunkel, *The Legends of Genesis: The Biblical Saga & History* . Trans. W.H. Carruth (NY: Schocken Books, 1964), p. 25. This wonderful little book is actually the introduction to Gunkel's magisterial 1901 commentary, *Genesis*. Trans. Mark E. Biddle. Mercer Library of Biblical Studies (Macon: Mercer University Press. 1997), pp. vii-lxxxvi.

3. Gunkel, *Legends of Genesis*, pp. 27-30.

4. Gunkel, *Legends of Genesis*, pp. 18-19.

5. *Gunkel, Legends of Genesis*, p. 134.

6. Gunkel, *Legends of Genesis*, pp. 30-34.

7. Gunkel, *Legends of Genesis*, pp. 34-35.

8. Burke O. Long, *The Problem of Etiological Narrative in the Old Testament* . Beihefte zur Zeitschrift für die alttestamentliche Wissenschaft 108 (Berlin: Verlag Alfred Töpelmann, 1968), provides very many examples from the Moses episodes. Gunkel hints at this in *Legends of Genesis*, pp. 35-36.

Chapter One

Moses, Get a Life!

Some recent scholars associated with the label "Old Testament Minimalism" are so radical in their estimate of biblical history as to deem everything up to the latest, most boring kings of Israel and Judah as legendary figments, pointing out the shocking absence of any archaeological evidence for the Exodus from Egypt or the temple of Solomon, or the monarchy of David. They include Thomas L. Thompson,[1] Philip R. Davies,[2] Mark Zwi Brettler,[3] Nils Peter Lemche,[4] and Giovanni Garbini,[5]

You don't need to be told what the implications of that viewpoint are for any historical Moses. I will not cover that ground. D.M. Murdock's recent book, *Did Moses Exist?*, takes a different approach, analyzing the telling parallels between the biblical Moses and the Greek god Dionysus, arguing that the former is a Hebrew version of the latter.

I second that motion, and I urge my readers not to miss that book. Mine might almost be considered an adjunct to her treatment of the subject. What I will do is to explain where, in the stark absence of facts, all that Moses material came from. This is the Moses compatible with Minimalism, the Moses who is merely a legal fiction.

But aren't there at least a few Moses tales which seem simply to tell the story of his life and serve no other purpose? What about the famous story of his nativity? As with so many biblical stories, there is both more and less than meets the eye. The "information" we seem to be getting turns out to be anything but factual, while the real agenda, at first unexpected, is quite fascinating.

Let's set the stage. As the curtain rises, we find a thriving colony of Israelites in Goshen, Egypt. They are the descendants of the extended family of the Patriarch Jacob and his dozen sons who arrived centuries ago as refugees from Canaan, where a famine raged. Once welcomed into Egypt, they have now become the object of paranoid suspicion on the part of the unnamed Pharaoh (Ramses II? Yul Brynner?) who fears their growing numbers and dreads the prospect of their some day becoming a fifth column to help invaders overthrow him. So he decides to cut off the population, telling the Hebrew midwives to kill any Hebrew male their mistresses produce.

We are already in Never-Never Land. Two midwives for a population so large that Pharaoh sees them as a dangerous threat? The fact that their names are given, Shifrah and Puah, implies we are not supposed to understand them as merely representative of a larger number, a whole profession. If we say that, we are not interpreting the story but rewriting it to suit us.

But the absurdities only multiply from there. How could the Pharaoh imagine such a plan could succeed? Even if the women were willing to carry out such orders, how could they hope to get away with it long enough to have access to any more babies? They'd have been out of a job the first time it happened. The parents are just not going to notice the midwives smothering their kids? Also, would Pharaoh have been fooled by such an obvious lie as the two midwives tell him? What they say implies that the Hebrews never need and thus do not have midwives.

If Shifrah and Puah are supposed to be Hebrews themselves (the Egyptian names tell us nothing, since Hebrews living in Egypt for many generations would be expected to give popular Egyptian names to their children), their excuse would be like a Hebrew baker explaining that Hebrews do not eat bread! If, on the other hand, the two women are Egyptians assigned by Pharaoh to act as midwives for the Hebrew women, there is still a problem: if there were no Hebrew midwives already on the job, shouldn't it have been obvious to Pharaoh that Hebrew mothers do not need them? This would have been like sending in a butcher to serve a vegetarian community.

So what is the point of the story? It is strictly a piece of comedy at the Pharaoh's expense: he is being depicted as a bumbling villain like Colonel Klink on *Hogan's Heroes*.

The nativity of Moses takes up Exodus 1:22-2:10:

> Then Pharaoh commanded all his people, "Every son that is born to the Hebrews you shall cast into the Nile, but you shall let every daughter live." Now a man from the house of Levi went and took to wife a daughter of Levi. The woman conceived and bore a son; and when she saw that he was a goodly child, she hid him three months. And when she could hide him no longer she took for him a basket made of bulrushes, and daubed it with bitumen and pitch; and she put the child in it and placed it among the reeds at the river's brink. And his sister stood at a distance, to know what would be done to him. Now the daughter of Pharaoh came down to bathe at the river, and her maidens walked beside the river; she saw the basket among the reeds and sent her maid to fetch it.

> When she opened it she saw the child; and lo, the babe was crying. She took pity on him and said, "This is one of the Hebrews' children." Then his sister said to Pharaoh's daughter, "Shall I go and call you a nurse from the Hebrew women to nurse the child for you?" And Pharaoh's daughter said to her, "Go." So the girl went and called the child's mother. And Pharaoh's daughter said to her, "Take this child away, and nurse him for me, and I will give you your wages." So the woman took the child and nursed him. And the child grew, and she brought him to Pharaoh's daughter, and he became her son; and she named him Moses, for she said, "Because I drew him out of the water."

Here we have an etymological legend intended to redefine the name "Moses." In this form, it is a fragment of an Egyptian name.[6] It means "begotten." It forms part of the theophoric ("god-bearing") names of the Pharaohs. "Ra*mses*" means "Ra has begotten him." "Thut*nose*" means "Thoth has begotten him."

Even in the story as it stands, it would make perfect sense for the character to have borne an Egyptian name, since he had been adopted into Pharaoh's household. But at some point, someone felt it unbecoming for the father of the Torah not to have a good Hebrew name, so this story serves to supply one. The story was not cut from whole cloth for this purpose; it has been borrowed from the far older nativity story of the Assyrian emperor Sargon. He, too, was set adrift in a river by his mother, who placed him tenderly in a basket crib she had fashioned from bulrushes. He, too, was retrieved from the water by a compassionate observer as the little boat drifted into view.

Well, if that was good enough for Sargon the Great, it was certainly good enough for Moses the Greater! But what has it got to do with Moses' name? Simply that the storyteller was looking for a possible Hebrew root word upon which "Moses" might be thought derivative. You see, Moses in Hebrew is Moshe, and that sounded close enough to the Hebrew word *mashah*, "to draw forth from." Well, if an infant's life had been saved by virtue of someone drawing him out of the river, that would be a pretty good reason to name him for it.

And notice the wonderful irony of the story! First, Moses' mother, after resigning herself to the loss of her infant son, gets to raise him after all, and she gets paid to do it, by the very people who had wanted the infant dead! And second, the very scheme intended to end the Hebrew threat to Egypt backfires royally, leading to the child Moses being taken into the very palace of the king of Egypt, from which he will eventually emerge to save Israel and level Egypt.

Just as the Gospels of Matthew and Luke skip from Jesus' childhood straight to his public ministry as an adult, leapfrogging the hypothetical events of his childhood and young adulthood, so does Exodus proceed directly from Moses' nativity to his adulthood. Just as the Apocryphal Infancy Gospels sought to fill Jesus' biographical vacuum with tall tales of childhood miracles, so did Josephus provide "information" on Moses' adventures as a loyal member of Pharaoh's court, and some of this made it onto the silver screen. But the Bible provides very little about Moses' life before God called him to liberate Israel. Where did this (scant) material come from? Mostly, it was borrowed from the Genesis stories of the Patriarch Jacob, Abraham's grandson. Consider these parallels between the biographies of Moses and Jacob.[7]

Moses Flees Eastward

Moses, living the high life as an Egyptian prince (I think we can assume a basic familiarity with the story up to this point, though we will return to it), already seems to harbor inklings of his future role as the Deliverer of the enslaved Israelites and makes a first, tentative strike in that direction. Happening to witness an Egyptian foreman abusing a Hebrew slave taking too long on his coffee break (or something), Moses whips out his knife and guts the oppressor. Looking in every direction to make sure no one saw the deed (though he is wrong), he consigns the corpse to a shallow grave in the sand.

But the next day, seeing two Hebrew slaves engaged in a shoving match, he intervenes, apparently already feeling his oats as a lawgiver and judge, only to have one of the men tell him to mind his own damn business. Did he plan to play judge, jury, and executioner like he did yesterday? *Uh-oh!* If this fellow knew, it couldn't take long to reach Pharaoh's ears. "Now when Pharaoh heard this thing, he sought to slay Moses. But Moses fled from the face of Pharaoh, and dwelt in the land of Midian: and he sat down by a well" (Exod. 2:15).

This anecdote will leave wide ripples in the scriptural pond. The words of the annoyed slave, "Who made you a judge over us?" appears again in Luke 12:13-14, where an irate man asks Jesus to arbitrate an inheritance dispute between him and his brother (things haven't changed much!). Jesus retorts, "Man, who made me a judge or divider over you?" (In

Saying 72 of the *Gospel of Thomas*, Jesus then turns to his disciples and asks, "I am not an arbiter, am I?") Also, in the legendary biography of the Prophet Muhammad, increasingly modeled on that of Moses,[8] he flees ambush in his home town of Mecca, taking in refuge in Medina, where he becomes their theocratic lawgiver. Sound familiar? "Midian" has become "Medina" with but a reshuffling of vowels (not original to either Hebrew or Arabic anyway).

But Moses' *hegira* (flight) to Midian is itself a literary echo of this episode from the saga of the Hebrew Patriarch Jacob (Gen. 27:41-45).

> Now Esau hated Jacob because of the blessing with which his father had blessed him, and Esau said to himself, "The days of mourning for my father are approaching; then I will kill my brother Jacob." But the words of Esau her older son were told to Rebekah; so she sent and called Jacob her younger son, and said to him, "Behold, your brother Esau comforts himself by planning to kill you. Now therefore, my son, obey my voice; arise, flee to Laban my brother in Haran, and stay with him a while, until your brother's fury turns away; until your brother's anger turns away, and he forgets what you have done to him; then I will send, and fetch you from there. Why should I be bereft of you both in one day?"

This is part of an elaborate ethnological story, explaining the historic bad blood between the kindred, neighboring Israelite and Edomite peoples (see, e,g., Psalm 137:7-9). The shrewd Jacob is the second born and the favorite of his mother Rebecca. She manipulates him into tricking his blind father Isaac to impart to Jacob the deathbed blessing that would seal the primogeniture rights of the first-born, namely Jacob's dim-witted brother Esau (destined to become the Edomite Patriarch).

Esau is old Isaac's favorite son, and he thinks he is blessing him, suspecting Isaac is putting one over on him but unable to prove it. When Esau finds out about it, he goes gunning for his brother, and their mother tells Jacob he'd better get out of town fast! Go east, young man! He does. Notice: Jacob is fleeing for his life, as is Moses when he heads east. No coincidence.

Moses Helps a Woman at a Well

The expatriate Moses finds himself cooling his heels at a well in Midian when a bevy of beauties arrive to water their father's flock. They wouldn't be doing this if they'd had any brothers to do the job. Their father, Reuel (from whom J.R.R. Tolkien derived his second middle initial), is keenly aware of this lack of a male heir, as we will soon see.

> Now the priest of Midian had seven daughters; and they came and drew water, and filled the troughs to water their father's flock. The shepherds came and drove them away; but Moses stood up and helped them, and watered their flock. When they came to their father Reuel, he said, "How is it that you have come so soon today?" They said, "An Egyptian delivered us out of the hand of the shepherds, and even drew water for us and watered the flock." He said to his daughters, "And where is he? Why have you left the man? Call him, that he may eat bread." And Moses was content to dwell with the man, and he gave Moses his daughter Zipporah. [Exod. 2:16-21]

This is what Robert Alter[9] (*The Art of Biblical Narrative*) calls a "type scene" that occurs again and again throughout scripture (see also Genesis 24 and John 4). Moses' sense of fair play, already displayed in his indignation over the mistreatment of the Hebrew slave, spurs him to challenge the bullies and make sure the seven sisters move to the head of the line. Because of this, they return home earlier than usual (which implies they always suffer such ill treatment from the local galoots).

Their father knows something is up. When he hears about the stranger who stuck up for his daughters, he sees his chance for a son-in-law. He has been as eager for one as the Russians for a warm-water port. They fetch their benefactor, and old Reuel offers Moses one of his daughters—and a job. He takes over as chief shepherd, leaving the girls to more conventionally feminine pursuits.

We need not chalk it up to synchronicity when we discover a closely parallel story about Jacob, and at precisely the same point in the story. He reaches his destination in the East, the land where his shifty uncle Laban lives, but he has not yet located the old man's dwelling. He rests at a well (an obvious choice for both stories, since any weary traveler is going to want a drink of water) and asks directions. And along comes his future bride (one of them, anyway):

> While he was still speaking with them, Rachel came with her father's sheep; for she kept them. Now when Jacob saw Rachel the daughter of Laban his mother's brother, and the sheep of Laban

> his mother's brother, Jacob went up and rolled the stone from the well's mouth, and watered the flock of Laban his mother's brother. Then Jacob kissed Rachel, and wept aloud. And Jacob told Rachel that he was her father's kinsman, and that he was Rebekah's son; and she ran and told her father.
>
> When Laban heard the tidings of Jacob his sister's son, he ran to meet him, and embraced him and kissed him, and brought him to his house. Jacob told Laban all these things, and Laban said to him, "Surely you are my bone and my flesh!" And he stayed with him a month. [Gen. 29:9-14]

Notice that this time there is but a single woman, as it happens, Laban's daughter, Jacob's cousin. She has a sister at home, but she is alone at the well. We have another version of Zipporah's predicament: Rachel, too, must wait till the other *male* shepherds have watered their flocks, but this time it's not a question of chauvinistic bullying. Rather, as a lone female, Rachel simply cannot lift the stone slab that covers the well. She has to wait for the more numerous and stronger males to do that, and it is only to be expected that those who take that trouble have first dibs on the water. Not unfair, but something of a predicament–until the mighty Jacob intervenes. There is only one of him, but he is able to lift the stone. (One wonders why he was afraid to match his strength against his brother's.)

Can this story be the literary origin of Mark 16:3-5, where a group of women (like Reuel's daughters) approach the tomb of Jesus, knowing they cannot roll aside the huge rock slab by themselves, only to find that a vigorous young man has done it for them? Remember, it's a type scene.

Again, the hero has met his mate, though not his only one: Jacob will wind up marrying Rachel's cross-eyed sister and (unofficially) Laban's two maidservants to boot. He's going to need them to produce the twelve sons who will in turn become the namesakes and progenitors of the twelve tribes. We may be sure that, had tradition traced a set of tribes to Moses (as it did to more ancient figures including Nahor (Gen. 22:20-24), Lot (Gen. 19:36-38), Ishmael (Gen. 17:20; 25:13-16), Seir (Gen. 36:20-28) and Esau (Gen 36:10-14)),[10] he would have married more of Reuel's daughters, too.

Moses Serves His Father-in-Law as a Herdsman

It is rather surprising that the subsequent Moses narrative does not take advantage of his description here as a shepherd. We do not read of his "shepherding the Israelite flock" subsequent to the exodus. The only function his brief shepherding career serves in the narrative is to get him to Mount Horeb, the Midianite Olympus, where God will reveal himself to Moses and give him his marching orders. Moses would have no business there, no reason to go there, except for the fact that his father-in-law moonlights as the priest of Midian by virtue of the circumstance that the sacred mountain falls within his grazing territory. His father-in-law is now called Jethro (for whom Jed Clampett's idiot nephew was named) because this portion of the story comes from a different source document than the one that knows him as Reuel. (Still another, in Numbers 10:29, calls him "Hobab.")

To digress to the Muhammad legend once more, let us not forget that the original name for Muhammad's refuge city of Medina, before they rechristened it in his honor ("Medina al Rasul," "City of the Prophet"), was Yathrib. That bears a suspicious resemblance to the Hebrew original of Jethro, "Yithro," with whom Moses allied himself after his hegira from Egypt. Again, no coincidence.

> Now Moses was keeping the flock of his father-in-law, Jethro, the priest of Midian; and he led his flock to the west side of the wilderness, and came to Horeb, the mountain of God. [Exod. 3:1a]

Genesis 29:18 tells us that "Jacob loved Rachel; and he said, 'I will serve you seven years for your younger daughter Rachel.'" He is as good as his word, as we later read: "Jacob said to him, 'You yourself know how I have served you, and how your cattle have fared with me'" (30:29). Again, we are building to an ethnological story that traces the tribes back to Jacob through his wives and concubines.

The whole thing is a fiction intended to seal the confederation of twelve originally independent tribes upon their coming together as religious, military, and economic allies, mirroring the ubiquitous Mediterranean pattern of the *amphictyony*,[11] a twelve (sometimes six) tribe league. Each member tribe took a monthly (or semiannual in the case of six tribes) turn staffing a central sacred sanctuary. The fictive sons of Jacob are *eponymous ancestors*, that is, imaginary "fathers of their countries" who, according to the text, bore the tribal names as their own personal names.

But the facts were just the other way around. The names were not personal names at first but had other denotations altogether. Some were geographical designations. "Benjamin" means "sons of the right hand," i.e., the south[12] (precisely the same as Yemen today on the southern coast of the

Arabian Peninsula). "Ephraim" (note the plural ending) means "dwellers on Mount Ephrath."[13] Others were the names of gods worshipped by a tribe. "Gad" was the Near Eastern god of good fortune.[14] "Zebulon" stands for Baal-Zebul, "Lord of the House," i.e., of the inhabited world[15] (a god mentioned in Mark 3:22). The tribe of Asher must have worshipped the goddess Asherah, prominent in the Old Testament, though she fell victim to the scissors of monotheistic editors.[16] Levi must have been named for the worship of the serpent deity Leviathan.[17] Still others denoted the traditional occupation of the tribe's members: "Issachar" means "burden bearers," just as "Hebrews" originally meant "migrant workers."

Garbini,[18] Lemche,[19] and other recent scholars have discarded the whole amphictyony hypothesis, and this seems to me one of the chief places where today's Minimalism clashes with the older paradigm of form-criticism (pursued here). Minimalism tends to dissolve as sheer fiction the historical circumstances that form critics have traditionally posited as the originary matrix for the creation of the various biblical stories. Minimalists effectively point out the astonishing lack of archaeological evidence for the traditional Old Testament history, as well as the fact that even "critical" histories of ancient Israel and Judah are little more than "rationalistic paraphrase" (Lemche)[20] of the Old Testament narrative. That is, the older critics tended to assume that the events recounted there did happen, minus the occasional miracle.

But it is not clear to me that the new approach is able to make the sense of much of the specific literary data that the form-critical paradigm does. The closing of the eyes to the manifest signs of oral tradition and its embellishment, as well as the sense the amphictyony model would make of the reinterpretation of tribal names, the trouble taken to posit a common ancestor, etc., reminds me of the obscurantism of the recent attempts to account for variations between the gospels in terms of the kind of oral ballad composition that Albert Lord[21] and Milman Parry[22] suggested for the Homeric epics.

The balladeer model simply chooses to ignore the patterns of redactional change delineated strikingly by Hans Conzelmann,[23] Günter Bornkamm, Gerhard Barth, Hans Joachim Held,[24] Willi Marxsen,[25] and others. As Thomas S. Kuhn[26] pointed out, if it is to succeed, a new paradigm must account for the familiar data accommodated by the paradigm it seeks to replace, and not just the new data of which its predecessor could make no sense. In the present book I am following the advice of Paul Feyerabend[27] to follow any hypothesis as far as it will go, as long as it is producing results, even if it is not yet clear how it comports with another hypothesis one is pursuing. That is perhaps the only way we will ever to be able to discover the outlines of a still larger paradigm where the various diverging trajectories will meet. Now we see in a glass darkly and must not, through a failure of nerve and patience, settle for premature closure. (How's that for harmonizing?)

Perhaps, though, Philip R. Davies[28] has indicated a promising direction when he posits the use of "genealogical codes" by Persian-era scribes as a means of accounting for the common worship of Yahweh by Jews and Edomites, Ammonites, Moabites, Transjordanians, and Samaritans. In other words, the use of fictive eponymous ancestors to negotiate the relations (however conceived) between groups implies something quite similar to what Gunkel posited re ethnological myths. Lemche [29] allows that the amphictyony system described by Noth is actually to be found in the texts. Noth wasn't hallucinating. His error, as Lemche sees it, was to take as genuine history a fictive model imposed retroactively by the biblical writers in order to provide an archaic, pre-monarchical history for their people. It seems to me that Lemche's reading, which makes sense to me, demands that tribal identity consciousness remained a concern of Jews even in the late, postexilic period, and that Davies and Lemche are essentially just moving the kind of process Gunkel described into a much more recent era than Gunkel imagined.

Sorry for the digression. The upshot is that the episodes contributing to Jacob's begetting of the twelve tribal Patriarchs are ethnological myths, not free fictional creations like a modern novel. By contrast, the corresponding Moses tales merely serve to move the narrative of Moses' adventures along.

God Appears and Tells Him to Return West

Exodus 3:1-10 ff. reveals what the whole shepherding thing was leading up to. It was a stratagem to get Moses up to the holy mountain where the Midianites believed God had his dwelling. But Moses' father-in-law did not send him there. No, Moses is simply in the vicinity, grazing the animals on the slopes of the mountain. Out of the corner of his eye he glimpses a strange sight: He sees a bush glowing, as if afire, though not collapsing into the inevitable ashes. This he's got to see!

> Now Moses was keeping the flock of his father-in-law, Jethro, the priest of Midian; and he led his flock to the west side of the wilderness, and came to Horeb, the mountain of God. And the

angel of the Lord appeared to him in a flame of fire out of the midst of a bush; and he looked, and lo, the bush was burning, yet it was not consumed. And Moses said, "I will turn aside and see this great sight, why the bush is not burnt."

Once he makes the ascent, and he hears the voice of Jehovah, we find two tokens of the ancient, robust belief that the presence of the Holy was nothing to take for granted. The voice instructs Moses to kick off his sandals because he now stands upon holy ground (though he must have known that already, as the son-in-law of the high priest of Midian, custodian of the Mountain of God). The idea is that profane footgear would ritually defile the holiness of the place. (Good thing his robe wasn't trailing on the ground, or he'd have had to stand there naked!) Or perhaps the holy radiation of the place would render the sandals sacred and thus unavailable for tracking back into the profane world outside.[30]

> When the Lord saw that he turned aside to see, God called to him out of the bush, "Moses, Moses!" And he said, "Here am I." Then he said, "Do not come near; put off your shoes from your feet, for the place on which you are standing is holy ground." And he said, "I am the God of your father, the God of Abraham, the God of Isaac, and the God of Jacob." And Moses hid his face, for he was afraid to look at God.

On top of that, once Moses knows this seeming freak phenomenon is actually the living presence of God, he averts his eyes. Why? Because, as we will later learn, "Man shall not see me and live" (Exod. 33:20). This motif appears variously throughout the Pentateuch (see Gen. 16:13; Exod. 19:21; 24:9-11; 33:11; Judg. 13:21-22), where sometimes people do manage to behold God and live to tell the tale, though they are surprised they did. The Medusa myth is probably a variation on the same theme, as is the belief that the sight of the god Pan would drive one mad ("panic").

But isn't there something of a contradiction in the story at this point? It is plain that Moses is seeing God himself, else why the holy terror? Yet the narrator says it was only the angel, i.e., messenger, who spoke from amid the flame. Elsewhere in the Old Testament as well as in neighboring Near Eastern mythology, angels were beings of blazing flame. So it makes sense.

Okay, you don't see angels every day, either. But the whole idea of angelic messengers would seem to presuppose that God wants to spare humans the deadly shock of a direct sight of himself. So Moses almost seems to be over-reacting (see Rev. 19:9-10). But that, again, seems to contradict the premise of the scene. What we most likely see here is the result of a squeamish scribe, writing from a later, more sophisticated perspective, who felt uneasy with the notion of God appearing in a particular place (like the local Baals who lurked in trees, springs, and oases) and speaking audible words.

At any rate, God tells Moses it is time for him to return home, back west, to finish the job he started when he disemboweled that Egyptian overseer. There will be plenty more where that came from! [31]

The corresponding Jacob story, upon which, again, the Moses version seems to be based, occurs in Genesis 31:13. A few chapters earlier (Gen. 28:10-22), on his way eastward, Jacob had spent the night out in the open, resting his head on the most uncomfortable pillow in history, a long, roundish stone. He wakes in a cold sweat from a dream in which he sees God's couriers going up and down a heavenly ladder or stairway, embarking on and returning from assigned missions. He realizes he has stumbled upon the very *axis mundi*, the place where heaven and earth, parallel planes, are joined like wheels on a common axis. [32]

God speaks to him in the dream, assuring him he will be with him and will fulfill the promises once made to Abraham that his progeny should one day inherit all of Palestine/Canaan. Knowing it for no mere dream, he takes it seriously as Freud or Jung would have, realizing that the place is, like Horeb, holy ground, whereupon he upends the cylindrical rock, pours oil atop it, and consecrates it as a *mazzebah*, or sacred pillar. [33] Henceforth travelers should know to watch their step, aware that they are passing over holy ground. He calls the new mini-shrine "Beth-el," "House of God," which may imply that originally the story supposed contact with the rock is what sparked Jacob's dream-vision of God because God lived in the rock. [34] It was literally the house of God/the god, a common enough notion in those days, albeit rather fetishistic. You can see how the story invited scribal or oral expansion to accommodate later belief.

The present passage alludes to that one: "I am the God of Beth-el, where you anointed a pillar, where you vowed a vow unto me: now arise, get out from this land, and return to the land of your nativity." So God reminds him on the way back home of the promise he made when Jacob was fleeing home, as if to remind the reader of what went before. But why bother locating the twin visions in this, or any, particular place? Simple. These (and other) anecdotes functioned as ceremonial myths to account for the choice of Bethel as the site of one of King Jeroboam's temples (1 Kings 12:28-29), in just the same way visitors to Glastonbury are told both that

Joseph of Arimathea had been there and that King Arthur and Queen Gwenivere were buried at the spot. The Moses version has no such prior tradition history.

Moses Returns with Wife and Child

The brief note in Exodus 4:20 informs us that Moses heeded God's command to return westward. "So Moses took his wife and his sons and set them on an ass, and went back to the land of Egypt; and in his hand Moses took the rod of God." It appears to be a simplified summary of Genesis 31:17-21, where his prototype Jacob did the same.

> So Jacob arose, and set his sons and his wives on camels; and he drove away all his cattle, all his livestock which he had gained, the cattle in his possession which he had acquired in Paddan-aram, to go to the land of Canaan to his father Isaac. Laban had gone to shear his sheep, and Rachel stole her father's household gods. And Jacob outwitted Laban the Aramean, in that he did not tell him that he intended to flee. He fled with all that he had, and arose and crossed the Euphrates, and set his face toward the hill country of Gilead.

Jacob had a bit of a history with his uncle Laban, somewhat reminiscent of Tony Soprano and his Uncle Junior. The upshot of all that was to provide an invidious caricature of the Aramaeans, of whom Laban is pointedly said to be one: shifty, exploitative, treacherous. In short, the Jacob version, of which the text reproduced here is but the iceberg tip, is another ethnological story, accounting for the traditional, "hereditary" enmity between the admittedly kindred nations of the Aramaeans and the Israelites. The Moses story lacks all that, or anything else like it, being merely a bit of transitional connective tissue.

God Ambushes Him

Perhaps the strangest of all biblical stories meets us in Exodus 4:24-26. Indeed, it seems almost to spring suddenly from the text to assault the reader just as the angry deity leaps from concealment to attack Moses!

> And it came to pass on the way at the lodging-place, that Yahweh met him, and sought to kill him. Then Zipporah took a flint, and cut off the foreskin of her son, and cast it at his feet; and she said,

Surely a bridegroom of blood art thou to me. So he let him alone.
Then she said, A bridegroom of blood art thou, because of the
circumcision. [Exod. 4:24-26, ASV]

What on earth is going on here? The placement of the episode is very nearly
as bizarre as the content of it. God, having just instructed Moses as to the
details of his mission, like M briefing James Bond, now mugs him like a
highwayman? He tries to kill the one he has chosen to liberate his people
from Egyptian captivity? Nor is it as if he means to tell him, as when God
pretended to command Abraham to slay his son Isaac, then told him it was
all a ruse (Gen. 22:12), for it says "he sought to kill him," that is, tried his
best to kill him.

Obviously it is some sort of primitive theological fossil, a religious
trilobite. But even at that, what does it mean, and what is it doing here? To
anticipate, we will at least be able to say that, unlike these other Moses
episodes parallel to Jacob episodes, this one does have a form-critical
fingerprint. That is, we can discern a prior *Sitz im Leben*, or ritual context
in which it originated. We can even think the thoughts of the editor that led
him to insert it where he did in the larger narrative.

There is a fascinating, if grotesque, discernible evolution in the Old
Testament from infant sacrifice to infant circumcision, and this zany Moses
tale can be confidently placed in that progression. One never hears sermons
on the shocking text of Exodus 22:29-30, "The first-born of your sons you
shall give to me. You shall do likewise with your oxen and with your sheep.
Seven days it shall be with its mother; on the eighth day you shall give
it to me."

The command is quite explicit: there is to be no difference between the
first son of each wife and the first-born of any female livestock. All alike are
to be slaughtered as a sacrifice to God, as a token of pious gratitude to God
who will bless this obedience by increasing the yield of these females
henceforward.

We know that ancient Israelites also sacrificed infants to Molech (or
Moloch), the charnel god whose fiery subterranean realm opened onto the
surface at Tophet, or Gehenna ("the valley of the sons of Hinnom") at the
base of Mount Zion (2 Kings. 23:10).[35] But these are not the sacrifices
stipulated in Exodus 22:29-30, which were pointedly commanded to be
offerings to Yahweh, Jehovah. As the morality of ancient Israel advanced,
many began to recoil from such barbarism. The prophet-priest Ezekiel
(20:25-26) sought to rationalize what he could not deny, having God

confess that he had ordered infant sacrifice as one of a set of laws meant to horrify Israel, though to what end is not quite clear. Some sort of wake-up call?

One of Ezekiel's priestly colleagues took a different approach in Exodus 13:12-13, reproducing the original commandment but adding the proviso that one might or must substitute an animal for the firstborn son, whom one rightfully owed to God. Why not simply omit the original command altogether in the new version of the Torah, the Priestly Code of which the Exodus 13 version formed a part? Too late for that. Remember Vatican II and the uproar occasioned by the Church changing all the old rules. The best the Priestly writer figured he could do was to mitigate it, leave the bomb on the ground but disarm it.

The famous story (Genesis 22) of the *Akedah Yitzakh* (sacrifice of Isaac) has been rewritten many times, having begun as a narrative account of the repeated but temporary supplanting of the sun (Isaac: "he laughs," referring to the beaming face of the sun) by the moon (Abraham: "father of a multitude," i.e., the moon, whose countless children are the smaller-seeming stars).[36] Eventually the story was repurposed to facilitate the transition effected by the revision of the firstborn sacrifice seen in Exodus 13, the substitution for a human baby by a newborn livestock animal.

Abraham is told to offer up his firstborn Isaac and nearly does so, and without any hint of the anxious inner torment ascribed to him by Kierkegaard. Of course: It was standard procedure in Israel. But God tells him to stay his hand as the knife begins its descent.

This version of the story is another version of a myth is which King Athamas, deceived by a false oracle, is about to sacrifice his son and heir Phrixus, only to be prevented by the sudden appearance of Hercules from heaven, who announces, "My father Zeus, King of Heaven, loathes human sacrifices!" whereupon the relieved lad hops aboard a mighty ram trapped in a nearby thicket and rides it to Colchis where Jason would one day venture to steal its golden fleece.[37] But in the Genesis version, the ram is sacrificed in a reapplication of the story, henceforth a ceremonial myth. Israelite fathers, follow the example of our common father Abraham! No more infant sacrifices! [38]

Archaic Israel, like other adjacent peoples, also practiced circumcision, only originally it was a puberty rite, "bridegroom circumcision." This version of the practice lingers in the story of Simeon and Levi in Genesis 34:15-16. For obvious reasons, puberty circumcision eventually gave way to infant circumcision. Let's get this over with, before a guy even knows he has a penis! Nothing to dread. And at that point, since all male babies were circumcised, the rite was reinterpreted as another way of substituting for infant sacrifice. The foreskin came to be understood as a token sacrifice of flesh.

Remember how in John 7:22-23 Jesus employs a similar logic: Though a Jew is not to work on the Sabbath, circumcision will proceed anyway if the boy's eighth day happens to fall on the Sabbath. How then can his critics criticize him for healing a man's whole body on the Sabbath? He presupposes that the foreskin is synecdoche for the entire body. And on the same terms, Exodus has God satisfied with the snipped foreskin of Moses' son Gershom in place of Moses' whole body, which God sought to harvest, presumably as punishment for his having neglected ever to get circumcised. He should have undergone the procedure before marrying Zipporah but did not. Now his baby son pays his debt, symbolizing the sanctioned replacement of bridegroom circumcision with infant circumcision. That is the form-critical significance of the story.

As to its location on the journey of Moses and his family from Midian to Egypt, we must suppose that this was simply the only available place, albeit an odd one, where it could fit. As incongruous as it is in the larger context, it is the only place where Moses is surrounded by his little family and not with the multitudes of Israelites, whether in the exodus from Egypt or wandering in the Sinai Desert. Why not just leave it out? No telling.

Matthew and Luke both found themselves affronted by Mark's stories of Jesus healing the sick by means of spit and polish (Mark 7:31-37; 8:22-26), no doubt because they made the Son of God look like some two-bit conjurer, and so omitted both from their own gospels. They each took over most of Mark's text, but these tales are conspicuous by their absence. Matthew and Luke's priority was damage control. On the other hand, some early scribe inserted the passage about the woman taken in adultery into John's gospel between what we count as 7:52 and 8:12. It was a free-floating Jesus story, and this scribe didn't want it to be lost, so he pinned it in what seemed to him a good juncture. He might as easily have done what Matthew and Luke did with the pair of embarrassing Markan stories, but instead, like the scribe copying John, he preferred not to lose any piece of sacred text. I doubt he even understood the ancient point of the story, but it was sacred material, so who was he to judge?

This tortuous tale is important for us, as we examinine the legendary life of Moses, because it shows this episode did have a pre-literary pre-history, unlike the others we have considered. Those seem simply to be rewrites of

Jacob stories, which did have a form-critical pre-history, left behind in the Moses versions, which function basically as biographical filler. And yet I maintain that the Moses story is still basically a copy of the Jacob story anyway; only in this case, Moses' hagiographer did not have to rewrite a Jacob story of God assaulting the hero. He had it already to hand and noticed the analogy between the Moses story and this one, the contest between Jacob and "the angel" in Genesis.

> The same night he arose and took his two wives, his two maids, and his eleven children, and crossed the ford of the Jabbok. He took them and sent them across the stream, and likewise everything that he had. And Jacob was left alone; and a man wrestled with him until the breaking of the day. When the man saw that he did not prevail against Jacob, he touched the hollow of his thigh; and Jacob's thigh was put out of joint as he wrestled with him. Then he said, "Let me go, for the day is breaking." But Jacob said, "I will not let you go, unless you bless me." And he said to him, "What is your name?" And he said, "Jacob." Then he said, "Your name shall no more be called Jacob, but Israel, for you have striven with God and with men, and have prevailed." Then Jacob asked him, "Tell me, I pray, your name." But he said, "Why is it that you ask my name?" And there he blessed him. So Jacob called the name of the place Peniel, saying, "For I have seen God face to face, and yet my life is preserved." The sun rose upon him as he passed Penuel, limping because of his thigh. Therefore to this day the Israelites do not eat the sinew of the hip which is upon the hollow of the thigh, because he touched the hollow of Jacob's thigh on the sinew of the hip. [Gen. 32:22-32]

This one has its own reason for being, or rather reasons, plural, since its tree-rings are readily discernible. On one level, it functions as an etymological myth to explain why Jacob bore two very different names, Jacob and Israel. My guess is that the point is to identify as one the mythic figureheads/ancestors of two groups of Hebrews. One traced their descent to Jacob, a sun god, the other to the epic hero Israel, who had bested a god in battle.[39]

Something similar had occurred in the unification of three Hebrew clans, one of whom worshipped "the God of Abraham," the second, a deity called "the Fear of Isaac" (Gen. 31:42), and a third, "the Mighty One of Jacob" (Gen. 49:24).[40] In that case, the result was a hierarchical rating of Abraham as the venerable grandfather, Isaac as the father, and Jacob as the son. This arrangement would have reflected the greater seniority, strength, and/or population of the three groups. But the Jacob and Israel groups either had already hit upon a different solution, according each's mythic forbear equal honor by amalgamating them, or the Israel group was a later addition to the Jacob group, intermarrying with them, too late for Israel to be factored into the now well established "Abraham-Isaac-Jacob" pantheon.

There is another etymological barnacle on this hull, seeking to re-explain the old place name "Peniel" ("face of God"), which must first have denoted simply that it was a sacred place of pilgrimage, where one sought the face of God in worship or seeking an oracle. But that wasn't good enough. Eventually someone's fertile imagination decided there must be more to it, and that the contest between Jacob and God/a god had taken place there. You can't help seeing the face of your opponent in a wrestling match. "Penuel" is a variant form of the same name. The fact that both occur here means that one is a subsequent addition by someone who was used to a different spelling.

This one, though, is a ceremonial myth. It takes off from the dirty trick used by Jacob's opponent to disable him, dislocating his thigh muscle, and uses it to rationalize a traditional dietary taboo against eating the corresponding muscle from any animal. This explanation may have replaced an earlier totemistic rule governing the annual devouring of a clan's patron animal.[41] Who knows?

Why had Jacob's opponent resorted to such a tactic in the first place? The intra-narrative motivation is that the sun is coming up and, like Dracula, the opponent cannot be found abroad in the light of day. That fits the folklore feel of the story. Even the notion of a god cheating in combat is familiar from Krishna clubbing a foe on the side of the knee in the *Mahabharata*. But I suspect the real reason is that the story teller has to justify the mention of Jacob's post-game limping because of what he wants to use it to explain/legitimatize: the ritual foot-dragging dance performed at Peniel, or as he knows it, Penuel.[42] We read that the priests of Baal performed just such a dance, "limping about the altar," in 1 Kings 18:26. Come on, baby, let's do the Limp.

Who was Jacob's antagonist? I read him as a local river god, that of the Jabbok, where the fight takes place. He would have been like the Trojan Scamander or a great number of others, named for the rivers they inhabit and protect. Notice the similarity between the names "Jabbok" and "Jacob"? They are constructed from the same tri-consonantal root, *jbk*. The river god is jealous of the name and fights Jacob for it. He wins, albeit by dubious means, and gives Jacob a fitting name to replace the one he has forfeited: "Israel," "One who fights with a god/God."

Of course, this story has been situated in a larger narrative context, where Jacob is understandably no longer understood to have endured a wrestling match with the Almighty. God-concepts have been elevated, while the titanic hero Jacob[43] has been cut down to size. Now, I believe, we are to read the story as a nocturnal encounter between Jacob and his alienated brother Esau, who turns out to be surprisingly willing to let bygones be bygones when the two meet officially the next morning.

What happened to Esau's seething hatred at being cheated out of his proper birthright? As I read it, Esau is willing to bury the hatchet—but not until he gets his long anticipated licks in! He sneaks up on Jacob the night before under cover of darkness and beats the hell out of him. His urgency to leave before the dawn is the result of his desire not to be recognized. He hopes to meet Jacob again with a clean slate a few hours hence. And when he does, his ruse has not succeeded, for Jacob wryly signals that he knows it was Esau who attacked him. If Esau had called Jacob a man able to fight with God, Jacob now quips that seeing Esau's familiar face is "like seeing the face of God." Namely, the one he had fought only hours before—his brother.[44] With a wink and an embrace, the brothers are reconciled. And, as we will shortly see, Moses has his own Esau to deal with, named Aaron.

Which cycle of tales was original, and which is the copy? I have suggested that the Jacob cycle came first, and this for two reasons. First, the Patriarchal traditions seem to have originated at an earlier point in Israelite history, representing the archaic period of "the gods of the fathers" posited by Albrecht Alt, when the God of Abraham, the Mighty One of Jacob, and the Fear of Isaac were separate totems of separate clans. These were combined later, once the three clans joined together and their eponymous ancestors, in order of clan seniority, were fictively made father, son, and grandson. I should imagine that these three gods of the clan patriarchs were originally Abraham, Isaac, and Jacob themselves.

It is evident from other stories featuring these characters, as we shall shortly see, that they were at first astral deities, Abraham being identified with the moon and paired with Isaac as the sun, Jacob as the moon set in opposition to Esau as the sun. Myths deified natural phenomena, only barely personifying them. As time passes, myths evolve into legends as their divine protagonists are demoted to demigods and culture heroes active on earth among human beings [45] in pseudo-historical times.[46] Thus the god

Abraham becomes the God of Abraham, as well as Abraham his servant. And eventually rationalistic scholars with residual religious loyalties will decide that a real, historical individual must have been the seed from which the legends grew, thus getting things exactly the wrong way round.[47]

Second, form-critically, when we examine the specific *raison d'être* of each story in each cycle, it looks as if each of the Jacob tales, prior to its inclusion in a connected sequence, had a distinct purpose (etymological, ethnological, ceremonial. etc.). By contrast, most of the Moses stories in this sequence seem to function simply to move the narrative along to the Exodus events, or to fill in the biography of Moses (perhaps to substitute for Moses' originally being an Egyptian, as Sigmund Freud[48] thought). With the exception of Exodus 4:24-26, the Moses episodes appear to have no form-critical prehistory, no function to account for their preservation and transmission. In short, the Jacob stories appear to be indigenous growths from various roots, not the result of copying from a prior source, while most of the Moses stories can be explained as copies since they do not serve other, prior, purposes.

Disclosure of the Divine Name

Exodus twice depicts God unveiling his true name, Yahweh, to supersede his former names *El Shaddai* (conventionally rendered as "God Almighty") and *Elohim* ("God," or "gods"). Moses is directed to inform the children of Israel of the preferred form of address. We find the Elohist version in 3:13-15, the Priestly version in 6:2-8.

> And Moses said unto God, Behold, when I come unto the children of Israel, and shall say unto them, The God of your fathers hath sent me unto you; and they shall say to me, What is his name? What shall I say unto them? And God said unto Moses, I AM THAT I AM: and he said, Thus shalt thou say unto the children of Israel, I AM hath sent me unto you. And God said moreover unto Moses, Thus shalt thou say unto the children of Israel, Yahweh, the God of your fathers, the God of Abraham, the God of Isaac, and the God of Jacob, hath sent me unto you: this is my name forever, and this is my memorial unto all generations. [Exod. 3:13-15, ASV]

> And God spake unto Moses, and said unto him, I am Yahweh: and I appeared unto Abraham, unto Isaac, and unto Jacob, as God Almighty; but by my name Yahweh I was not known to them. And I have also established my covenant with them, to give them the

land of Canaan, the land of their sojournings, wherein they sojourned. And moreover I have heard the groaning of the children of Israel, whom the Egyptians keep in bondage; and I have remembered my covenant. Wherefore say unto the children of Israel, I am Yahweh, and I will bring you out from under the burdens of the Egyptians, and I will rid you out of their bondage, and I will redeem you with an outstretched arm, and with great judgments: and I will take you to me for a people, and I will be to you a God; and ye shall know that I am Yahweh your God, who bringeth you out from under the burdens of the Egyptians. And I will bring you in unto the land which I sware to give to Abraham, to Isaac, and to Jacob; and I will give it you for a heritage: I am Yahweh. [Exod. 6:2-8, ASV]

One has to suspect that what we are witnessing here is the programmatic attempt to merge two hitherto-distinct deities, just as in Genesis 14:19-22, Yahweh is said to be another name for the Most High God (i.e., the king of the gods), *El Elyon.* In all these cases, what poses as an indicative ("God has various names, you know.") is really an imperative ("From now on, thou shalt consider these gods as the same."). It was once theorized that Israel adopted the Kenite deity Yahweh from the Kenite tribe, historically allies of Judah. If we accepted the story of Moses' relationship to Jethro, the priest of Midian, it would be a very natural hypothesis, Yahweh being the local god whom Jethro served. But the later, historical Kenite-Judah link would make the adoption of Yahweh just as natural. But it now develops that Yahweh was a good deal more available than that. He had not been the exclusive property of Judah.

John Day[49] thinks this unification of gods occurred as of the addition of the conquered Jebusite city-state (Jeru)Salem to the Davidic empire, whereupon David and his heirs took over the prior Melchizedek priesthood. He considers Elyon the Jebusite deity, Yahweh the Judean, and that the two had to be fused for religious and political reasons, as if Constantine had elected to conflate the Christian God with Sol Invictus, whose pontiff he was. This theory illustrates the difficulty posed for even recent scholarship by the advent of Minimalism, for it now seems that what once seemed to be historical landmarks, among which we sought to situate various myths and sagas, are fully as fictive. We often seem to be working in a vacuum.

At any rate, now we can explain much more naturally a minor puzzle over which older scholars[50] deliberated: why the biblical Yahweh appeared to combine features of the Canaanite gods El and Baal. The answer is simple once one realizes that Yahweh and Elyon, like their alter egos Baal and El, were originally separate gods but, in Israel, were later combined.

Why is there no Yahwist (J) version of the changeover of the names? Simply because the J writer had long since taken for granted the merger of the underlying deities. To him, Elohim and Yahweh had always been two aliases for the same God. We might compare him to the authors of Acts, 1 Peter, and 2 Peter, who were merging Paulinist and Petrinist forms of Christianity,[51] producing works in which the two rival factions either (as with E and P) are harmonized on the page before us or (as with J) are depicted as if there had never been a hatchet to bury in the first place. (What this implies for the relative dating of the J, E, and P sources, I leave to others to figure out.)

Adventures in the Pest Zone

Moses is the central figure, or rather one of a duo of central figures, in the story of the devastating plagues. There is in effect a second Moses in the story, namely Aaron. Where did he come from? Back when Jehovah was prepping Moses for his mission of liberation, Moses was less than self-confident, objecting that he possessed no eloquence and could scarcely serve as God's spokesman to the elders of Israel, much less deliver thundering ultimatums to Pharaoh. God assures Moses that he will back him up when the time comes (as in Luke 21:12-15), but Moses is still chicken. Running out of patience, God proposes sending Moses' brother Aaron, who has the gift of gab, to be Moses' press secretary.

This is obviously an attempt to put Moses in the shade.[52] Aaron just does not fit into the story and has been forced into it like a square peg in a round hole.[53] For one thing, his presence in the plague narratives seems totally superfluous. Sometimes it is Moses who calls down the plagues and makes demands of Pharaoh; sometimes it is Aaron. Thus Aaron seems solely to be stealing a bit of Moses' thunder, and only by virtue of "me-too-ism."

Some readers may be old enough, and to have wasted enough time, to remember the transitional period between *The Andy Griffith Show* and its lame successor, once Andy retired, *Mayberry RFD*, starring Ken Berry. For one season, Andy and Ken appeared side by side in every episode, Ken merely echoing everything Andy said and did. If Andy tried to persuade Goober not to do something, Ken would add his two cents, really the same two cents. The producers were thereby trying to acclimate us to Ken Berry as the second Andy so we'd still tune in after Andy left. He was like a video ghost of Andy on an old TV set with bad reception. That's Aaron: a superfluous double of Moses.

When we first see Aaron, it is during Moses' sojourn in Midian, right before Moses takes Zipporah and young Gershom with him to Egypt, and Aaron just walks on stage from the wings (Exod. 4:27). Wait a second! Moses had a brother? Was there a second basket floating down the Nile? Did Pharaoh's daughter fish baby Aaron out, too? And what was he doing in Midian? Did he follow Moses there, too? There's certainly no hint of it in any of the prior stories.

And later on we meet Moses' equally unanticipated sister, Miriam (probably originally a water nymph or a music goddess akin to the Near Eastern music god Jubal, who appears in Genesis 4:21 as the culture hero who invented music, like Apollo.[54] Here we have something of an analogy to the New Testament problem of the brothers and sisters of Jesus (Mark 6:3). Christian theology puzzled over how the only-begotten Son of God could have mortal siblings. Moses, too, seems intended as a unique figure, the only son of Amram and Jochebed, who brought him into a hostile world at great risk. For him suddenly to have a brother and sister seems like a subsequent embellishment. And it is.

Aaron appears to be the invention of the later Aaronic priesthood, a fictive eponymous ancestor who functions to give their order equal status with the scribes who took Moses as their model. We see the same priestly revisionism in the Book of Chronicles, a tendentious (ax-grinding) rewrite of part of the Deuternomic (or, if you prefer more syllables, Deuteronomistic) [55] History, namely the Books of Samuel and Kings. In the priestly version, priests figure as important characters, even heroes, in the stories, where their presence was unhinted before. They are feathering their own nests. Moses is supposed to be descended from the priestly tribe of Levi, but it seems that others had claimed him, and the priests felt the need to create their own Moses analogue to elevate their own status.[56]

In some ways, as we shall see, Moses was a royal figure. In Post-Exilic Judaism, with independence a thing of the past, there were no more Jewish kings. During this time the newly-minted High Priestly office replaced that of the old kings, the High Priest appropriating many of the kings' domestic functions and even their distinctive vestments. It may be that the priests regarded Moses (with his implicit royal authority) as obsolete (though their rivals, the scribes, continued to exalt him) and sought to supplant him with their own hero, inserting him alongside Moses in the original stories. The

Priestly source was not the only set of Moses stories used to compile the
Pentateuch, so many stories remain in which Moses is at center stage, the
star of the show.

Moses' continued but vestigial presence in the Priestly stories in Exodus
is a prime example of Martin Noth's [57] redundancy principle. If a character
remains onstage but is not in the spotlight, we have to wonder what he is
doing there at all, and we may infer that he has been shouldered aside by
the redactor who feels no need to erase him but wants to assign a superior
role to a new favorite. There was no reason to eliminate Moses, after all. He
hadn't become a villain.

But there is reason to apply the redundancy principle to Moses himself,
as Noth did. Doing so would effectively remove him from the original
version of the saga of the plagues—and maybe everything else! When Moses
and his sacerdotal sidekick arrive in Egypt and contact the elders of Israel,
persuading them to unionize and present their demands to Pharaoh
(Exod.5:15-21), we are surprised to read that Moses and Aaron wait in the
hall outside while the elders go before Pharaoh to make their case. When
Pharaoh dismisses them scornfully, Moses and Aaron rush over and ask,
"Well, how did it go?" If we follow Noth's redundancy principle we would
have to ask if Moses and Aaron had originally been the stars of the show,
but that someone has shoved them aside in favor of the unnamed and
colorless group of Israelite elders.[58] But what if this is a case of what Mark
C. Goodacre [59] calls "editorial fatigue," a case of a redactor "nodding" over
his work, neglecting the pattern of reworking his sources that he has
otherwise pursued systematically.

For example, the redactor/compiler of Luke-Acts seems to have wanted
to eliminate the notion of Jesus' death having redemptive significance
(seeing it rather as a prophesied martyrdom pure and simple). He
eliminated the references to Jesus giving his life as a ransom (compare
Luke 22:20a with Mark 14:24 and Luke 22:27 with Mark 10:45) and has
Peter preach that repentance and baptism in Jesus' name are what saves,
with no mention of a redemptive death, only a predicted one (Acts 2:38;
3:19). But then he has Paul refer to God/Christ "buying the church with his
own blood" (Acts 20:28). Oops! Likewise, Matthew seems to have wanted,
out of pious decorum, to replace all of the references to "the kingdom of
God" that he found in his sources with the equivalent phrase "kingdom of
heaven." But there are a few places where he didn't (Matt. 12:28; 19:23, 24;
21:31, 43). Just missed them.

If you have ever proofread something only to notice goofs in the printed copy, you know how easy it is to succumb to editorial fatigue. That's what seems to have happened in Exodus 5:15-21. Noth reasons that the passage is a vestige of an earlier version in which all the plague stories featured the group of elders confronting Pharaoh and calling down the plagues when he refuses their demand. Moses, not to mention Aaron, would not yet have been added to the story. Once the redactor did insert them all across the story, he just missed this one, thinking it adequate to leave it as it originally read since it was now surrounded by episodes featuring Moses and Aaron. This does not bode particularly well for a historical Moses. And, as we will see, most of the wilderness stories make pretty good sense without Moses, too.

As everyone knows, there are ten plagues in the Exodus narrative, but originally it was not so. Our Pentateuchal text is a compilation of sources, and there appear to have been separate accounts of the Egyptian plagues in three of them. The J source has a sequence of seven plagues (a number that nobody is surprised to see in the Bible): water turning to blood, frogs, flies, cattle slain, hail, locusts, and the death of the firstborn. Whoever wrote Psalm 78 knew this version of the story, as he recounts only these. The E source had the water changing to blood, the hail, the locust invasion, and the death of the firstborn, then adds the plague of dense darkness. The P source had the water turning to blood, the frog infestation, the death of the firstborn, and adds an infestation of gnats and an outbreak of boils. Psalm 105 seems to reply upon our combined version, though it does not mention every single one of the plagues.

Apologist K.A. Kitchen,[60] quixotically seeking to overthrow the JEDP hypothesis, argues in the manner of the eighteenth-century Protestant Rationalists who (rather perversely to our ways of thinking) insisted that scriptural narratives, though not miraculously inspired, were nonetheless accurate, stemming from eyewitnesses (a purely *ad hoc* hypothesis, as it remains today). The Rationalists, good scientific Newtonians, embraced the notion of a clockwork universe in which God did not stop the clock to work intrusive miracles, suspending natural law. So they posited that the ancients, inevitably ignorant of science, jumped the gun, attributing astonishing events to supernatural miracles.

These moderns thought they could vindicate the biblical accounts, ironically, by cooking up some rationalistic, scientific explanation for what must *really* have happened. Whether Kitchen adhered consistently to a Rationalist position or not, he adopted their methods about Exodus, arguing that most of the plagues were really natural phenomena that commonly occurred together in linked sequence in ancient Egypt. When the Nile floods each year in August, the water can turn red from the presence of microscopic flagellates, which poison the fish. Then, in September, there is sometimes a huge influx of frogs, fleeing the river banks because of the rotting fish floating there. But this amphibian exodus would be too late, since the croakers would soon expire from anthrax contracted from the fish. The excess water would form an ideal breeding ground for flies and mosquitoes. These bugs would spread varieties of anthrax to humans (hence the boils) and cattle (killing them). The same rains that caused the flood would tend to invite swarms of locusts. And the "thick darkness" might denote a subsequent dust storm from the drying up of the excess alluvial mud.

Why not? And the pay-off? The sequence works only if all these plagues occur together in the story. If we divide the plague narrative into these sources with their partial lists, the natural sequence is broken, and one can no longer make the plagues out to be scientifically explicable natural phenomena.

But this strikes me as a peculiar, even circular, way to argue. Kitchen assumes that any explanation that makes the Bible more historically credible is to be preferred. And then he goes on from there to show that such a reading of the text rescues it not only from skepticism-inviting supernaturalism but from dissection into prior sources as well. Why is either preferable?

There are other problems lurking with the attempt to rationalize the miracle-story of the plagues. For one thing, hail storms are not common in Egypt.[61] For another, the interpretation of the thick darkness as a dust storm or sand storm seems gratuitous and *ad hoc*: If something really happened there, which the apologist wants to believe, then this is the best bet. And there is the irony implicit in the whole Rationalist approach: The apologist (explicitly in the old days, implicitly and unnoticed today) has to sacrifice the miraculous in order to vindicate the Bible as accurate. Just not an accurate account of miracles, which would seem to be the point of inerrancy apologetics, no? [62]

But, perhaps worst of all, if Kitchen is right, it is not simply that the ancient "observers" would have failed to understand the science behind what they were seeing. That is like Joseph F. Blumrich[63] arguing that the prophet Ezekiel beheld a space shuttle landing on the banks of the Chebar in Babylon and described it as the throne-chariot of Jehovah, since that was the only conceptual category he could squeeze it into. The premise, not a silly one, is that an ancient man did his best to describe a marvel that he could not begin to understand in scientific terms. (Whether it happened or not is of course quite a different question.)

No, Kitchen's scenario is very, very different. He is implying that the biblical writer was so far removed from the events that he did not recognize the plagues, which any ancient Egyptian or Hebrew would have,[64] as the familiar effects of the annual flooding of the Nile. The writer clearly knew little about Egypt. If he had been anywhere near the place, whether in space or time, he wouldn't have needed to blow up the events into mythical miracles. He wouldn't even have thought them extraordinary, any more than a Florida resident is surprised to encounter a bout of 100 MPH winds and torrential rains during hurricane season.

Whence the idea of the plague narrative? I would venture that it has grown from the more modest tale of Abram and Sarai's sojourn in Egypt in Genesis 12:10-20. We find a variant version of the same story over in Genesis 20, where the more familiar forms of their names, Abraham and Sarah, are used, and they sojourn in Philistine Gerar, of whose king Abimilech they run afoul. There is a third version (Gen. 26:6-16), this time starring Isaac and Rebecca (because someone repeating the story couldn't remember which patriarch was featured), again traveling to Gerar and meeting Abimilech.

Just as when jokes circulate today people unwittingly change character names and locations, all such features being secondary to the plot and punch line, these episodes are all variations on the theme that the patriarch visits a foreign land with his beautiful wife and, in order to save his yellow hide, claims she is his sister in case the king spots her and wants to add her to his seraglio. At least that way the king won't have him killed to get to her! He should have trusted God and didn't, but now God is going to take care of them anyway. He speaks in a dream to the heathen king, warning him to keep his mitts off the patriarch's wife. The king is happy to do so but rebukes the patriarch for getting him into trouble with God. Now knowing Abram/Abraham/Isaac for God's favorite, he loads him down with goodies and kicks him out. "Here's your burnoose; what's your hurry?"

How did Abimelech turn into Pharaoh? Not as a nod to the Exodus story, which I am suggesting did not yet exist, but rather simply through a natural—one might even say *inevitable*—confusion between the Muzrim, the group of Philistines to whom Gerar belonged, and Mizraim, the Hebrew name for Egypt. (Remember, there were originally no vowels!). Once the land of the Muzrim became Mizraim, Abimelech was "corrected" to the

Egyptian *Pharaoh*.[65]

The biblical compilers did not feel free to leave any of the versions out since each must have been the favorite of some readers/hearers. Think of children who will brook the omission of no detail of a favorite bedtime story.[66] They had to fit them into a larger narrative where ever they could. And this explains some of the unwittingly hilarious contradictions in the jerry-rigged narrative. Imagine Pharaoh drooling over Sarah, who according to an earlier but originally unrelated story (Gen. 17:17), must be above ninety years old! Hubba hubba.

Is the Exodus story of Moses and the plagues a fourth version of the same story? Do we not begin to feel a bit of *deja vu*[67] when we read that God punished Pharaoh's lust for Sarai with "great plagues"? Wait a minute. . . *Pharaoh*? *Plagues* as a means to extricate a couple of *Hebrews* from *Egypt*? What's going on?

Here's an idea. Someone was looking to enhance the story of the Israelite exodus from Egypt, which had originally depicted the Israelites sneaking out of an untroubled Egypt. The episode of Pharaoh's overtaking the children of Israel at the Reed Sea[68] would make more sense if Pharaoh had not known his slaves were departing until they were gone, then sought to recover them.[69] The artificiality of Pharaoh repeatedly agreeing to let Moses' people go, then reneging, is obvious, and the narrator, to account for it, simply has God say he is going to hypnotize poor Pharaoh again and again so as to deal out enough rope for him to hang himself.

It is not unlike the passion predictions of Jesus in the gospels (Mark 8:31; 9:9, 31; 10:33-34): The narrator means to reassure, not the characters on the scene, but rather his readers,[70] that Jesus knew his destiny and would not be taken by surprise. But since he has had to have Jesus say it in the presence of his ubiquitous disciples, he has to account for the fact that they will be totally taken by surprise when it actually happens. So he simply says, by authorial fiat, that they did not understand his plain speech (Mark 9:10, 32; Luke 18:34).

I suggest that our Exodus narrator derived the notion of God's pummeling Pharaoh into submission from the Abram, Sarai, and Pharaoh story. From that point, the story of the plagues itself spread and varied in the telling, which is why we find slightly different J, E, and P versions now stitched together in Exodus. At any rate, it is just a story, not a report, since, as we have seen, whoever told it had no real idea of conditions in Egypt. This may be where that story originated.

And it shall be, when Yahweh shall bring thee into the land of the Canaanite, as he sware unto thee and to thy fathers, and shall give it thee, that thou shalt set apart unto Yahweh all that openeth the womb, and every firstling which thou hast that cometh of a beast; the males shall be Yahweh's. And every firstling of an ass thou shalt redeem with a lamb; and if thou wilt not redeem it, then thou shalt break its neck: and all the first-born of man among thy sons shalt thou redeem. And it shall be, when thy son asketh thee in time to come, saying, What is this? that thou shalt say unto him, By strength of hand Yahweh brought us out from Egypt, from the house of bondage: and it came to pass, when Pharaoh would hardly let us go, that Yahweh slew all the first-born in the land of Egypt, both the first-born of man, and the first-born of beast: therefore I sacrifice to Yahweh all that openeth the womb, being males; but all the first-born of my sons I redeem. [Exod. 13:11-15, ASV]

Passover was originally a shepherd's feast, the Feast of Firstlings, when one would sacrifice the firstborn lambs of each ewe in gratitude to one's god for a good livestock yield. Originally it had nothing to do with commemorating the exodus from Egypt. The text itself makes this clear, since the Hebrews are portrayed as already accustomed to celebrating it (3:18). We have independent evidence that ancient Bedouins observed the feast in the desert as well.

Shepherds worshipped what we call the planet Venus (known in the Bible as Helal, son of Shahar, the Dawn Goddess) or the moon. Desert shepherds herded their flocks in the cool of the night, beneath the moon and stars, shunning the bitter radiance of the unforgiving desert sun. One sacrificed the firstborn lambs or camels and consumed them ritually, sharing the banquet with the deity, in whose presence the meal was to be eaten. It had to be eaten in haste and finished by sunrise, because then the greater light of the sun would obscure the lesser light of the moon (or Venus, cf. Isaiah 14::12-15).

There are obvious similarities to the rules for Passover, which was celebrated at the full moon (Exod. 12:8), implying that the Hebrews (some Hebrews) had earlier worshipped the moon (as Father Abraham) with this ceremony. They had to finish it before sunrise (Exod. 12:9-11). How did this feast get connected with the exodus story? It became part of the narrative in order to give it a new legitimization at a subsequent historical period when the desert days were a remote memory.

How about the detail of the daubing of blood on the doorposts (Exod. 12:27)? This, too, was a common Near Eastern custom, still observed today,[71] whereby people will slaughter a goat or a sheep and brush the blood on the doors of a new house. They hope thus to placate God (or the *djinn*, basically the Grim Reaper) or to secure the protection of Saint George, on the assumption that sooner or later death will visit every home, and they are trying to "get it over with" by killing an animal, so no member of the family will have to die somewhere down the line. The blood tells the angel of death "I gave at the office." The Hebrews/Israelites eventually decided this practice needed to be provided a good Jewish explanation, so they told the story of the Passover lamb to explain (or re-explain) it (Exod. 12:26-27).

The same is true of the concurrent Feast of Unleavened Bread (Exod. 13:3-8). Exodus 12:34, 39 is a ceremonial story told to explain (or re-explain) an already ancient harvest feast. The first of the wheat crop to come to maturity was offered in its pure form, unmixed with leaven, to one's god in the same spirit as the firstlings of the flock, in gratitude, hoping that the deity would reward the offering with "more from where that came from." Linking it with Moses gave the practice a secure footing in the Torah. So now we read that the bread lacked leaven because the people had packed up their kitchens and were poised to evacuate Goshen at any moment, ironically, a measure of purely secular expedience.

Fuzzy Math

As for the rest of the Exodus, two observations are necessary. First, archaeology rules it out. There is simply no evidence of such a mass migration of refugees and animals anywhere in the Sinai desert. Various possible routes for the exodus have been proposed, but, pick whichever one you prefer, there is no evidence. Keep in mind that investigators now use infrared aerial scanning techniques that can spot hitherto-invisible caravan trails in the Sinai Desert used in ancient times, like an exterminator using an ultraviolet lamp to expose rat urine trails. And they show no trace of the exodus.

There is no way around this for Bible accuracy partisans. They now find themselves in the same leaking boat with the poor Mormons, who have never been able to turn up a trace of the once-mighty Nephite and Lamanite civilizations described in the Book of Mormon. What can have happened? Did God send down a bunch of angels with vacuum cleaners to remove the evidence, like sanitation workers cleaning up after a ticker-tape parade? You might as well believe that Satan planted dinosaur bones to disturb the faithful.

Second, as Bishop Colenso[72] showed long ago, the Exodus story is statistically impossible. Exodus implies an Israelite population of some two million strong. Colenso shows how, marching fifty abreast in formation (though obviously the mass of people would have sprawled out and taken more room), the column of fleeing Israelites would have stretched for about twenty-two miles! They are said to have brought with them herds of cattle— into a "howling desert"! Where do you suppose Moses and Aaron found provender for the animals, much less food for the people? As we will see, the people occasionally get hungry enough to complain, but this must have been the rule, not the exception, with so many people in an arid waste. Their encampment would have covered an area of some twelve square miles, and keep in mind one had to use a pooper- scooper to dispose of one's excrement outside the borders of the camp (Deut. 23:12-14). Who was more anal-retentive: the priests who were such sticklers for detail, or the fictional Israelites they imagined keeping their rules?

This populace should contain some 600,000 potential fighting men, who, according to Exodus 13:18 and Joshua 4:12, were well-armed. This is a mighty host indeed! What need, then, to fear the approach of Pharaoh's troops, whom they would have outmanned and outgunned? Why had they not risen up to throw off the Egyptian yoke long before? And, as miserable slaves, where could they have obtained these weapons? Forget it.

The Exodus narratives have God not merely give to Moses a code of laws that will govern settled agricultural existence in the Promised Land once they get there. No, we read that the Israelite refugees are to start living by them at once, in the wilderness. They must build a tabernacle (or "tent of meeting") to carry with them. It is so elaborate in design and detail that, as Julius Wellhausen noted,[73] it cannot ever have existed in such circumstances (just imagine knocking it down every morning to lug it through the desert!) and represents instead an attempt to read a miniature version of Solomon's Jerusalem temple back into the sacred time of origins, the days of Moses.

The idea was to give it a Mosaic pedigree once such things had come to matter. Well, we read that Moses would periodically summon "the whole congregation" of Israel to impart new revelations or directions. Colenso bids us try to picture a vast multitude of two million people gathering around this tent. Someone just failed to think this through.

When Colenso starts tabulating the sacrifices of various types that the desert-dwelling Israelites were required to offer (wherever they got the animals!), compared with the staff of three sacrificing priests (Aaron, Eleazer, and Ithamar), it becomes downright hilarious. Such a population must have produced, on average, 250 childbirths every day, and each birth required two sacrifices (a burnt offering and a sin offering), hence 500 sacrifices each day. As stipulated in the text, each such offering must have taken at least five minutes apiece. It would have taken the trio of priests about 42 hours in a 24 hour day to get through it, and that's with no coffee breaks or trips to the bathroom!

Similarly, Colenso pictures the observance of Passover at Sinai in Numbers 9:5, which would have required the priestly trio to sacrifice some 150,000 lambs (and to sprinkle the blood) for the two million people within the stipulated twenty-four hours. Dividing the butchery between the three of them, that comes to four hundred lambs per minute!

And there is much more. In all this, Colenso has merely troubled to notice what most Bible readers had never possessed the patience or the interest to do: crunch the numbers and see if they really add up. They don't. The logistical problems attaching to the exodus from Egypt easily rival those of the Noah's ark myth.

Red Sea Pedestrians

To grasp what is going on in the famous story of the dryshod crossing of the Reed Sea, we must acquaint ourselves with the important mytheme upon which it is based, that of Yahweh as the Divine Warrior.[74] Have you ever read the Noah story and wondered why God would, as a token of his promise never again to flood the human race out like rats, place "his bow" in the sky? Of course, every reader recognizes the rainbow when one appears. Indeed this portion of the Noah story is an etiological myth "explaining" to a pre-scientific audience the origin of the rainbow.

Nowadays we know that the rainbow appears once the rain has pretty much stopped; the diffused water vapor lingering in the air acts as a prism refracting the re-emerging sunlight. But the ancients couldn't know that, so they imagined the rainbow appeared just before the rain stopped. It was the reminder for God to turn off the spigot so the world would not float away again. But wait a second—God's bow? What sort of a bow would he have, and how would he use it?

There is ample evidence demonstrating that, precisely like his Canaanite and Syrian counterparts, Aliyan Baal and Baal Hadad, Yahweh was a storm god and a war god. The two go together for obvious reasons: thunder sounds like the clashing of combat in the skies, and the lightnings look like (and often strike like) dangerous projectiles. They are the arrows God dispatches from his mighty war bow. This he does while riding to war in his cloud chariot. Like Baal, he is the "rider of the clouds" (e.g., Pss. 68:4, 17). He is "the Lord of Hosts," i.e., commander of the heavenly armies. And, in the aftermath of the Flood, he has made peace, swearing never to resume the combat through which he had slaughtered the bulk of the human race. He has hung up his gloves, or his guns, as we might say.

The Old Testament fairly teems with allusions to the wars of Yahweh, marching from the south, from the mountains of Edom, to fight for his people Israel against their enemies (see Gen 32:2-3; Deut. 33:2-5; 26-29; Judg. 5; Psalm 68; Exod. 15; 2 Sam. 5:22-25 22:7-18, Josh. 5:13-15; 10:12-13; 2 Kings 6:15-19; 7:6; Isa. 13:1ff; 40:26; 45:12; Zech. 14; Hab. 3:3-15). As Patrick D. Miller, Jr., observes, while the imagery closely matches that of the Baal myths of Canaan and the Marduk myths of Babylon, there is a important difference: While Baal marshals his forces against rival gods and monsters, Yamm, Mot, and Lotan, and Marduk rallies his troops against the divine monsters Tiamat, Apsu, and Kingu, Yahweh fights earthly enemies, the nations opposed to Israel.

I think Miller exaggerates the difference, since there are plenty of Old Testament references (Job 3:8; 7:12; 9:5-14; 38:8-11; 40:15-41:26; Ps. 65:7-8; 74:12-17; 89:10-15; 93; 104:1-9; Isa. 51:9-11, etc.) to the mythical combats of Yahweh against the Chaos dragons Leviathan (= the Canaanite Lotan), Tannin, Behemoth, and Rahab.[75] But he is correct in drawing attention to the application of the Divine Warrior mythos to Israel's earthly wars. It was part and parcel of the institution of Holy War[76] (a doctrine still causing plenty of trouble today as Jihad).

The way I read Miller is promoting the party line of the 1950s-60s "Biblical Theology" movement inspired by G. Ernest Wright.[77] These scholars rode the old theological hobby horse of Israel's supposed "radical" difference from the pagan peoples around her.[78] There is something that today's readers ought to keep in mind that has not been clear until recently. Traditionally, even critical studies, still very useful, have operated under the sway of the old-time apologetical view that Israel was a distinct people who, upon entry into Canaan under Joshua's leadership, engaged in syncretism, assimilating heathen notions and myths from the few Canaanites they neglected to exterminate.

Now, though, it has become clear that the Israelites were simply one more group of native Canaanites who had never been in Egypt. Their religion was simply their local version of the Canaanite religion. They didn't, and didn't have to, "borrow" anything from "those Canaanites." The "people of the land" was just the way later priests and reformers pejoratively described adherents of the "old-time religion" who refused to "get with the program"—if they even knew about it.

However, let it be noted that the notion of Israel's borrowing from the indigenous Canaanites becomes newly viable on another Minimalist theory, namely that Judah essentially began as a Persian province populated by deportees from unknown parts whom the Persians resettled (a systematic policy for dealing with conquered subjects) in a Palestine that had never been home to them or their ancestors. To make the new arrivals feel at home there, scribes in the employ of the Persians would have fabricated a sacred history of the resettled colonists' supposed ancestors in the newly settled territory which made it sound like the settlers were returning to an ancient homeland from which their ancestors had been previously exiled. This would have been the origin of the biblical story of Israelite origins.[79]

And this composition might well have involved wholesale borrowing from the indigenous inhabitants. In fact we have something close to a forthright depiction of this scenario in 2 Kings 17:24-34. Nor was it only deportees whom the Persians relocated in this manner. They did the same thing with laborers on long-term projects.[80] In light of this fact, perhaps we ought to take a second look at the proposed etymology of "Hebrews" as meaning "migrant workers."

The way the Biblical Theology Movement scholars saw it, the heathen Canaanites held to a static worldview based on a cyclical recurrence of Sacred Time. Every year, the Near Eastern kings reenacted the myth of Marduk's or Baal's primordial combat with the monsters of chaos and his triumph and subsequent creation of the world from his foes' carcasses. The king was the god's vicar on earth, and his annual victory in this miracle play renewed both his right to rule with delegated divine authority and the tenuous vitality of the earth. It was a religion of cosmic maintenance, of the status quo.

By contrast, they said, the biblical, Israelite worldview was linear, beginning with God's creation (even if it did involve a battle with the chaos monsters, though this element has been largely bowdlerized by the time of J's creation, the Garden of Eden myth, and P's seven-day creation). God reveals himself in the dynamic forward trajectory of a history whose events are to be interpreted as "the mighty act of God" on Israel's behalf, including the exodus and the conquest of Canaan (though he could also acts in judgment if his covenant people proved disobedient).

This was, it turned out, a rather selective reading of scripture. It seems that the difference between the two models was not so very great after all. The Bible itself took for granted that the gods of the nations performed "mighty acts" on behalf of their clients, as when Jephthah acknowledges that Chemosh, the patron deity of the Ammonites, had given them their land just as Yahweh had allotted Palestine to Israel (Judg. 11:24). Chemosh later intervenes (2 Kings 3:26-27) on Moab's behalf, vanquishing Israel's troops!

Paul D. Hanson[81] sliced the pie differently, demonstrating that, though all Israelites/Jews accepted the mythical scenario whereby Yahweh was a Divine Warrior who smote Leviathan and Rahab to establish his throne, competing factions applied it differently in their polemics against one another. Whoever was currently in power stressed Yahweh's annually renewed victory as guaranteeing the status quo, which they enjoyed. Whoever was then out of power accentuated the battle motif to claim that God was fighting, as he had at the dawn of time, on their behalf in the current struggle—or they hoped he would and prayed for the day of victory. So it was often a more intra-Israelite contrast between the cyclical reinforcement of a divine status quo versus the invocation of the Divine Warrior to fight new battles against one's rivals.

Mircea Eliade, in *The Sacred and the Profane*,[82] showed how all ancient cultures believed that Profane Time was linear and would roll on meaninglessly, like a run-on sentence, except that it is periodically intersected (punctuated, so to speak) by the "eternal return" of Sacred Time, which is indeed cyclical, the sacred/mythic time of origins mystically returning every year to renew the expiring creation. The Biblical Theology Movement might better have adopted Eliade's distinction, admitting that Israel (the Bible), as well as the adjacent heathen, operated within linear Profane Time punctuated by the occasional intrusion of Sacred Time, the guidance and intervention of God or the gods.

This would have made more sense of what is otherwise an odd contradiction in the Biblical Theology model, namely that Wright, Von Rad, and the rest did not actually think there had *been* any supernatural interventions of God, only that the ancient Israelites thought there had been and ritually commemorated them in a "theology of recital." One of the Biblical Theology Movement's hallmarks was to posit a distinction between

Heilsgeschichte, Salvation History, on the one hand and ordinary, factual history on the other. That distinction would seem to fit Eliade's schema perfectly, *Heilsgeschichte* corresponding to the purely mythic Sacred Time invoked in ritual.

For the Biblical Theology Movement, the ostensible "mighty acts of God" had occurred in the realm of faith, not that of real history. They were what theologian Gordon D. Kaufman called the Easter morning hallucinations of the disciples of Jesus: "events in the history of meaning." [83] It is just the same difference Paul Veyne indicated in the case of the ancient Greeks who believed the exploits of Zeus, Athena, and Heracles had happened—*sort of*.

The Israelites were careful not to regard their victories as their own doing. "Lest Israel vaunt themselves against me, saying, 'My own hand has delivered me"(Judg. 7:2). So they gave the glory to God who had granted the victory. And in time this self-effacement led to a wholesale mythologization of the great triumphs of the past, making Israel pretty much passive witnesses of God's overt miracles as he led his heavenly hosts against Pharaoh and subsequent heathen foes. At length the poetry of piety turned into prose. This, as I read him, is just the approach Miller takes in his study of Yahweh as the Divine Warrior in Israel.

And I think, again, that he has it exactly backwards. He and his colleagues are indulging in *euhemerism*, the ancient assumption that every myth has a basis in fact, so that, e.g., war gods were once flesh-and-blood warriors. The Storm God was at first merely Stormin' Norman! We must instead begin with the myth and trace its concretization into this-worldly history. And this is nowhere clearer than in the case of the Reed Sea crossing. Exodus 15 presents the already ancient poem known as the Song of Moses (or the Song of the Sea), a commemoration of the victory of Yahweh over Pharaoh's army. But maybe that's putting Pharaoh's chariot before his horse.

> And Yahweh spake unto Moses, saying, Speak unto the children of Israel, that they turn back and encamp before Pihahiroth, between Migdol and the sea, before Baal-zephon: over against it shall ye encamp by the sea. And Pharaoh will say of the children of Israel, They are entangled in the land, the wilderness hath shut them in. And I will harden Pharaoh's heart, and he shall follow after them; and I will get me honor upon Pharaoh, and upon all his host: and the Egyptians shall know that I am Yahweh. And they did so.

And it was told the king of Egypt that the people were fled: and the heart of Pharaoh and of his servants was changed towards the people, and they said, What is this we have done, that we have let Israel go from serving us? And he made ready his chariot, and took his people with him: and he took six hundred chosen chariots, and all the chariots of Egypt, and captains over all of them. And Yahweh hardened the heart of Pharaoh king of Egypt, and he pursued after the children of Israel: for the children of Israel went out with a high hand. And the Egyptians pursued after them, all the horses and chariots of Pharaoh, and his horsemen, and his army, and overtook them encamping by the sea, beside Pihahiroth, before Baal-zephon.

And when Pharaoh drew nigh, the children of Israel lifted up their eyes, and, behold, the Egyptians were marching after them; and they were sore afraid: and the children of Israel cried out unto Yahweh. And they said unto Moses, Because there were no graves in Egypt, hast thou taken us away to die in the wilderness? wherefore hast thou dealt thus with us, to bring us forth out of Egypt? Is not this the word that we spake unto thee in Egypt, saying, Let us alone, that we may serve the Egyptians? For it were better for us to serve the Egyptians, than that we should die in the wilderness.

And Moses said unto the people, Fear ye not, stand still, and see the salvation of Yahweh, which he will work for you to-day: for the Egyptians whom ye have seen to-day, ye shall see them again no more for ever. Yahweh will fight for you, and ye shall hold your peace. And Yahweh said unto Moses, Wherefore criest thou unto me? speak unto the children of Israel, that they go forward. And lift thou up thy rod, and stretch out thy hand over the sea, and divide it: and the children of Israel shall go into the midst of the sea on dry ground. And I, behold, I will harden the hearts of the Egyptians, and they shall go in after them: and I will get me honor upon Pharaoh, and upon all his host, upon his chariots, and upon his horsemen.

And the Egyptians shall know that I am Yahweh, when I have gotten me honor upon Pharaoh, upon his chariots, and upon his horsemen. And the angel of God, who went before the camp of Israel, removed and went behind them; and the pillar of cloud removed from before them, and stood behind them: and it came between the camp of Egypt and the camp of Israel; and there was the cloud and the darkness, yet gave it light by night: and the one came not near the other all the night.

And Moses stretched out his hand over the sea; and Yahweh caused the sea to go back by a strong east wind all the night, and made the sea dry land, and the waters were divided. And the children of Israel went into the midst of the sea upon the dry ground: and the waters were a wall unto them on their right hand, and on their left. And the Egyptians pursued, and went in after them into the midst of the sea, all Pharaoh's horses, his chariots, and his horsemen. And it came to pass in the morning watch, that Yahweh looked forth upon the host of the Egyptians through the pillar of fire and of cloud, and discomfited the host of the Egyptians. And he took off their chariot wheels, and they drove them heavily; so that the Egyptians said, Let us flee from the face of Israel; for Yahweh fighteth for them against the Egyptians.

And Yahweh said unto Moses, Stretch out thy hand over the sea, that the waters may come again upon the Egyptians, upon their chariots, and upon their horsemen. And Moses stretched forth his hand over the sea, and the sea returned to its strength when the morning appeared; and the Egyptians fled against it; and Yahweh overthrew the Egyptians in the midst of the sea. And the waters returned, and covered the chariots, and the horsemen, even all the host of Pharaoh that went in after them into the sea; there remained not so much as one of them. But the children of Israel walked upon dry land in the midst of the sea; and the waters were a wall unto them on their right hand, and on their left.

Thus Yahweh saved Israel that day out of the hand of the Egyptians; and Israel saw the Egyptians dead upon the sea-shore. And Israel saw the great work which Yahweh did upon the Egyptians, and the people feared Yahweh: and they believed in Yahweh, and in his servant Moses. [Exod. 14, ASV]

This, as Miller demonstrates, is classic Divine Warrior mythology. But was it inspired by real events? Is it not a more economical explanation to posit that the prose miracle story of chapter 14 is built up from this typical piece of epic/hymnic poetry? [84] Egypt is once called "Rahab" in the Bible (Pss.

87:4).[85] This is no coincidence. Isaiah 51:9-10 invokes the myth of Rahab (the same as Leviathan), the primordial dragon killed by Yahweh (Pss. 89:10; Job 9:13; 26:12), applying it to the return of Jews from the Babylonian Exile.

We are in the habit of reading the passage as comparing both the exodus from Egypt and the return from Babylon to the whelming of Rahab, but I am not so sure any reference to Egypt was intended. The reference in verse 10 to the drying up of the seabed must originally have referred to the drying up of the primeval ocean, personified by the sea dragons Rahab and Leviathan. The "redeemed" should not be too quickly read in light of the exodus of Hebrew refugees from Egypt but may instead have referred to the gods whom Yahweh (like Marduk) had rescued by his victory. Once the raging ocean was bound in its place, dry land became available (Gen. 1:9-10; Job 38:8; 11; Pss 104:5-9)–to gods and men alike.

I suggest that later readers lost sight of the consistently mythic reading and began to see a reference to the Egyptian exodus at the Reed Sea. The name "Rahab" came in this way to be applied to Egypt. Continuing the trajectory, the Exodus 14 lyric simply introduces the names Pharaoh and Egypt.

Why steer around this obvious inference with the needlessly elaborate theory that something big *did* happen between Israel and Egypt at the Reed Sea, and then it was blown up into the Song of Moses by way of adapting the stock mytheme of the Divine Warrior? Why not eliminate the middle-man? Straight from the myth to the pseudo-historical legend, the same progression evident everywhere else as we see gods demoted to heroes who stride the earth among men. It seems altogether arbitrary to see it going the opposite direction, and over the bridge of hypothetical but unknown mundane events.

Must we be hell-bent, like the old Protestant Rationalists, on preserving some pitiful, factual core to the myth? If the exodus itself left none of the traces it must have left had it occurred, the story of the Reed Sea must vanish along with it.

I am with Noth[86] when it comes to the secondary role, not only of Aaron, but even of Moses in the narrative of the plagues. It is already evident that Moses and Aaron are each redundant to the other, and really neither one is needful. As it was the anonymous elders of Israel who made demands of Pharaoh in the name of their God in Exodus 5:15-19, we must suspect that it was the same voices that reiterated them, and called down the plagues, throughout the story. Only subsequently did Moses attain prominence and find his way into the stories. To jump ahead, it seems quite likely that Moses debuted only in the Sinai story in which he originally figured as a sun god who gave laws to his people, just like Apollo and Shamash.

Astute readers may be scratching their heads and asking themselves, "Wait a second! If the story of the Israelites leaving Egypt is fiction, how did they get back to Canaan?" Well, it is quite simple to extricate yourself from somewhere you have never been in the first place. And that is the case here.

How strange that the Hebrews lived in Egypt, in Goshen, for fully four centuries before Moses led them out—and yet nothing, not a minute of that period, about twice the length of the history of the United States, is recorded! Did nothing of note, not a single event worthy of mention, transpire during that whole time? No, the Hebrew sojourn in Egypt is just as arbitrary a fiction as the thousand-year Reich of the Messiah Jesus in Revelation 20:6-7, "Blessed and holy is he who shares in the first resurrection! Over such the second death has no power, but they shall be priests of God and of Christ, and they shall reign with him a thousand years. And when the thousand years are ended, Satan will be loosed from his prison," etc. A millennium passes between two sentences! So it is with the four centuries in Goshen. There simply was no story to tell. The Millennium hasn't happened yet; the sojourn in Egypt never happened at all.

Then why did anyone ever say it did? Garbini[87] suggests that the whole business originated during the time Judea was part of the Ptolemaic Empire of Egypt, post Alexander the Great. Jews flourished under that regime, before they got handed off to the tyrannical Seleucid Empire. They found it politic to create an origin myth whereby they originated in Egypt and only later moved en masse to Palestine. Or, as Davies[88] suggests, it may be that the core of the exodus story was the return of Palestinian (presumably including Jews/Israelites) troops formerly garrisoned in Egypt by their Assyrian masters. Letters home (unearthed at Elephantine) indicate they were not treated well there by the locals who resented their presence, and they finally had enough and left.

Notes

1. Thomas L. Thompson, *The Mythic Past: Biblical Archaeology and the Myth of Israel* (London: Basic Books, 1999).

2. Philip R. Davies, *In Search of Ancient Israel*. Journal for the Study of the Old

Testament Supplement Series 148. (Sheffield: Sheffield Academic Press, 1992);

3. Mark Zvi Brettler, *The Creation of History in Ancient Israel* (London: Routledge, 1998).

4. Niels Peter Lemche, *The Israelites in History and Tradition*. Library of Ancient Israel (Louisvelle: Westminster John Knox Press, 1998).

5. Giovanni Garbini, *History & Ideology in Ancient Israel* (NY: Crossroad, 1988).

6. Martin Noth, *A History of Pentateuchal Traditions*. Trans. Bernhard W. Anderson (Englewood Cliffs: Prentiss-Hall, 1972), p. 159.

7. Robert Graves and Raphael Patai. *Hebrew Myths: The Book of Genesis* (NY: Greenwich House, 1983), p. 229.

8. Patricia Crone and Michael Cook, *Hagarism: The Making of the Islamic World* (NY: Cambridge University Press, 1977), Chapter 3, "The Prophet Like Moses," pp. 16-20.

9. Robert Alter, *The Art of Biblical Narrative* (NY: Basic Books, 2nd ed., 2011), Chapter 3, "Biblical Type-Scenes and the Uses of Convention," pp. 55-78.

10. Martin Noth, *The History of Israel* (London: SCM Press, 1983), p. 87.

11. Noth, *History of Israel*, pp. 85-109.

12. Ignaz Goldziher, *Mythology Among the Hebrews and its Historical Development*. Trans. Russell Martineau (1877; rpt. NY: Cooper Square Publishers, 1967), pp. 175-176.

13. Goldziher, p. 175.

14. Goldziher, p. 176.

15. William Menzies Alexander, *Demonic Possession in the New Testament: Its Historical, Medical, and Theological Aspects* (Edinburgh: T&T Clark, 1902; rpt. Grand Rapids: Baker Book House, 1980), pp. 181-182.

16. Raphael Patai, *The Hebrew Goddess* (NY: Discus/Avon Books, 1978), pp. 16-41.

17. Goldziher, pp. 183-184. Michael D. Goulder (*The Psalms of Asaph and the Pentateuch*. Studies in the Psalter, III. Journal for the Study of the Old Testament Supplement Series 233 (Sheffield: Sheffield Academic Press, 1996), pp. 68-71) shows that Leviathan (the Canaanite Lotan, Baal's opponent) was the personification of the Litani River of Syria-Lebanon. In its winding course, it received numerous tributaries, which suggested the seven heads of the dragon. Thus there is the thinnest of lines between the texts in which Yahweh (like Baal) defeats Yamm, the personified sea, and those in which he crushes the heads of Leviathan. (Remember, the name of the Greek Hydra, so similar to Leviathan, simply means "water.")

18. Garbini, p. 123.

19. Lemche, pp. 97-102 .

20. Lemche, pp. 148-156; Garbini, p. 21.

21. Albert Lord, *The Singer of Tales*. Harvard Studies in Comparative Literature, 24 (Cambridge: Harvard University Press, 1981).

22. Milman Parry, *The Making of Homeric Verse: The Collected Papers of Milman Parry* (NY: Oxford University Press), 1987.

23. Hans Conzelmann, *The Theology of St. Luke* Trans. Geoffrey Buswell (NY: Harper & Row, 1961).

24. Günter Bornkamm, Gerhard Barth, Hans Joachim Held, *Tradition and Interpretation in Matthew*. Trans. Percy Scott. New Testament Library (Philadelphia: Westminster Press, 1963).

25. Willi Marxsen, *Mark the Evangelist*. Trans. James Boyce, Donald Juel, William Poehlmann, Roy Harrisville (NY. Abingdon Press, 1969).

26. Thomas S. Kuhn, *The Structure of Scientific Revolutions* (Chicago: University of Chicago Press, 1962), pp. 24-25

27. Paul Feyerabend, *Against Method* (NY: Verso, rev. ed. 1988), p. 27.

28. Davies, pp.79, 85.

29. Lemche, pp. 104-107.

30. It's a funny thing how the ancient categories of ritual pollution seem to meet in the middle, with mundane things becoming "unclean" upon contact with the holy. Mary Douglas summarizes one understanding of the matter (though her own is more complex, too elaborate to pursue here): "the universe is divided between things and actions which are subject to restriction and others which are not; among the restrictions some are intended to protect divinity from profanation, and others to protect the profane from the dangerous intrusion of divinity." *Purity and Danger: An Analysis of Concepts of Pollution and Taboo* . Penguin Anthropology Library (Baltimore: Penguin Books, 1970), p. 18. One might have expected that the holiness of a sacred object would rub off on even the profane hand which rudely touched it, but it is instead rendered "profane." In such cases the contracted profanity seems to stand for the supernatural damage incurred in judgment, however that danger is understood. We find this concept in 1 Corinthians 11:29, "Anyone who eats and drinks [holy communion] without discerning the body [of Christ] eats and drinks judgment upon himself."

31. See Luke 13:1-5.

32. Mircea Eliade, *The Sacred and the Profane: The Nature of Religion* . Trans. Willard R. Trask (NY: Harcourt, Brace & World, 1959), pp. 38-39; Richard J. Clifford, *The Cosmic Mountain in Canaan and the Old Testament* . Harvard Semitic Monographs Volume 4 (Cambridge: Harvard University Press, 1972; rpt. Eugene: Wipf and Stock Publishers, 2010); E. Theodore Mullen, Jr., *The Assembly of the Gods: The Divine Council in Canaanite and Early Hebrew Literature*. Harvard Semitic Monographs Number 24 (Chico: Scholars Press, 1980), pp. 128-132, 146-160.

33. W. Robertson Smith, *Lectures on the Religion of the Semites. First Series: The Fundamental Institutions*. Burnett Lectures 1888-89 (London: Adam and Charles Black, 1914), pp. 203-204; Helmer Ringgren, *Israelite Religion*. Trans. David E. Green (Philadelphia: Fortress Press, 1966), pp. 24-25.

34. Robertson Smith, pp. 204-205.

35. John Day, *Molech: A God of Human Sacrifice in the Old Testament* . University of Cambridge Oriental Publications No. 41 (NY: Cambridge University Press, 1898).

36. Goldziher, pp. 32, 45-47, 92-96,.

37. Graves and Patai, p. 176.

38. Gunkel, p. 31.

39. Garbini, p. 80.

40. Albrecht Alt, "The Gods of the Fathers." In Alt, *Essays on Old Testament History and Religion*. Trans. R.A. Wilson (Garden City: Doubleday Anchor Books, 1968), pp. 1-86.

41. Robertson Smith, pp. 286-311.

42. Gunkel, *Legends of Genesis*, p. 31.

43. Gunkel, *Legends of Genesis*, p. 120.

44. Actually, Esau *was* a god, a sun god (of which many national mythologies seem to possess several). His name means "red" (a common sun god epithet), and he is said to be hairy (Gen. 25:25), a trait which, as with his solar colleagues Samson (Judg. 17:17, 19) and Elijah (2 Kings 1:1:8, literally, "he was a hairy man"), denotes the rays of the sun (Goldziher, pp. 134-144, etc.). He was the not-quite eponymous ancestor of the Edomites, but the Bible does not call him "Edom." But there had been an Edom character. The Edomites would have viewed him as both their nation's progenitor and that of the human race as a whole since, as many ancient peoples did, they would have imagined themselves as the root stock of the human race. For some reason the ancient Hebrews borrowed him (more interesting myths?) to serve as their own "first man" character. "Adam" would seem to be but a slight variant of "Edom" (like "Carl and Charles"), especially when we recall that these languages had no consistent vowels, only written consonants. In a classic instance of Noth's redundancy principle at work, we still find the original Hebrew "first man" character on stage but elbowed to the side: Enosh (which means "man," cf. *bar enosh* or *bar nasha*, "the son of man") in Genesis 4:26; 5:6.

45. Jaan Puhvel, *Comparative Mythology* (Baltimore: Johns Hopkins University Press, 1987), p. 139. Puhvel is discussing Indo-Euopean mythology, but the same pattern seems to appear in other mythologies as well.

46. Paul Veyne, *Did the Greeks Believe in their Myths? An Essay on the Constitutive Imagination.* Trans. Paula Wissing (Chicago: University of Chicago Press, 1988), p. 80: "the Greeks held their gods to be true, although these gods existed for them in a space-time that was secretly different from the one in which their believers lived."

47. The biblical Samson is transparently a Hebrew sun god. His very name means "the sun"! And yet Jacob M. Myers, "The Book of Judges: Introduction and Exegesis," *The Interpreter's Bible*, II (NY: Abingdon-Cokesbury, 1953), p. 776, opines that "While it cannot be doubted that *some legendary accretions* have attached themselves to the tales, there can be little hesitancy in regarding Samson as a historical personality." Some legendary accretions? One might as

well say Paul Bunyan was a historical personage. Rather, one ought to face the facts: "almost everything that is told about these characters is only an empty tale, but the total of these zeroes makes a positive sum" (Veyne, p. 50). We will see that the same is true of Moses.

48. Sigmund Freud, *Moses and Monotheism*. Trans. Katherine Jones (NY: Vintage Books, 1939, 1967), Part II. "If Moses Was an Egyptian," pp. 16-65.

49. John Day, *God's Conflict with the Dragon and the Sea: Echoes of a Canaanite Myth in the Old Testament*. University of Cambridge Oriental Publications No. 35 (NY: Cambridge University Press, 1985), pp. 130-131.

50. Mullen, *Assembly of the Gods*, p. 156 creates a problem where none exists by insisting that Elyon was from the first merely an epithet of the Hebrew Yahweh (pp. 204-205). The generation of scholars influenced by William Fozwell Albright and Frank Moore Cross wanted ancient Israel, not just later Judaism, to have been monotheistic.

51. Ferdinand Christian Baur, *Paul the Apostle of Jesus Christ: His Life and Works, his Epistles and Teachings*. Trans. Edward Zeller (London: Williams and Norgate, 1873-1875; rpt. Peabody: Hendrickson Publishers, 2003), pp. 196; 250-251; Baur, *The Church History of the First Three Centuries* . Trans. Allan Menzies. Theological Translation Fund Library (London: Williams & Norgate, 1878). Vol. I, pp. 128-136.

52. See the same phenomenon in Matthew's treatment of Peter. Arlo J. Nau, *Peter in Matthew: Discipleship, Diplomacy, and Dispraise* (Collegeville: A Michael Glazier Book/Liturgical Press, 1992). Mark had sought to discredit Peter (i.e., the bishops who claimed succession from him), and the first "Matthew," using Mark's gospel, rewrote passages to rehabilitate Peter's reputation. But a subsequent Matthean redactor fiddled further with the text in order to take Peter back down a peg.

53. Noth, *History of Pentateuchal Traditions*, p. 162.

54. Goldziher, pp, 129-130.

55. There is a technical distinction between these two terms if one wants to maintain it. "Deuteronomic" properly refers to features of the Book of Deuteronomy, while "Deuteronomistic" refers to the work of the compilers of the so-called Deuteronomistic School who compiled the "Deuteronomistic History" known to us as Joshua, Judges, 1 and 2 Samuel, and 1 and 2 Kings.

56. Noth, *History of Pentateuchal Traditions*, p. 30, note 14, observes how Aaron is a subsequent insertion even in the J narratives.

57. Noth, *History of Pentateuchal Traditions*, pp. 71, 156-166.

58. Noth, *History of Pentateuchal Traditions*, p. 163.

59. Mark C. Goodacre, "Fatigue in the Synoptics," *New Testament Studies* 44 (1998), p. 45.

60. K.A. Kitchen, *Ancient Orient and Old Testament* (London: Tyndale Press, 1966).

61. Noth, *History of Pentateuchal Traditions*, p. 69.

62. James Barr pointed this out years ago in his classic work *Fundamentalism* (Philadelphia: Westminster Press, 1976), pp. 241-242.

63. Joseph F. Blumrich, *The Spaceships of Ezekiel* (NY: Bantam Books, 1974).

64. Noth, *History of Pentateuchal Traditions*, p. 69, theorizes that the description of conditions in Egypt reflects the "rather general knowledge" that Israelites had accumulated from traveling merchants, but this would scarcely account for the utter ignorance implied by the conditions being depicted as supernatural miracles and therefore anything but standard and recurring weather.

65. Gunkel, *Legends of Genesis*, p. 102.

66. And who can blame them? I bristled when I noticed that syndicated reruns of *The Sopranos* were missing some of my favorite scenes, so I broke down and bought the DVDs.

67. Or, if we speak Klingon, *nipoch*.

68. The Hebrew has *Yam Suph*, "Sea of Reeds," not the Red Sea, which is a larger body of water. It was the translators of the Greek Septuagint who changed it to "Red Sea," perhaps because they were aware that the shallow water of the Yam Suph could not be pictured as being made to stack up as walls of water.

69. Noth, *History of Pentateuchal Traditions*, p. 70.

70. Robert M. Fowler, *Let the Reader Understand: Reader Response Criticism and the Gospel of Mark* (Minneapolis: Fortress Press, 1991).

71. Samuel Ives Curtiss, *Primitive Semitic Religion To-day: A Record of Researches, Discoveries and Studies in Syria, Palestine and the Sinaitic Peninsula* (NY: Fleming Revell Company, 1902), pp. 184, 216, 224-227.

72. John William Colenso, *The Pentateuch and Book of Joshua Critically Examined* (NY: D. Appleton, 1863).

73. Julius Wellhausen, *Prolegomena to the History of Ancient Israel*. Trans. Menzies and Black (NY: Meridian Books/World Publishing, 1957).pp. 34-38.

74. Regarding the heading "Red Sea Pedestrians," see Graham Chapman, John Cleese, Terry Gilliam, Eric Idle, Terry Jones, Michael Palin, Monty Python's *The Life of Brian (of Nazareth)* (NY: Ace Books, 1979), p. 31.

75. The classic treatment of this mytheme is Hermann Gunkel's 1895 study *Schöpfung und Chaos in Urzeit und Endzeit: Eine Religionsgeschichtliche Untersuchung über Gen. 1 und Ap. Jon 12,* or *Creation and Chaos in the Primeval Era and the Eschaton: A Religio-Historical Study of Genesis 1 and Revelation 12*. Trans. K. William Whitney, Jr. Biblical Resource Series (Grand Rapids: Eerdmans, 2006). See also a most helpful follow-up study, John Day, *God's Conflict with the Dragon and the Sea: Echoes of a Canaanite Myth in the Old Testament*. University of Cambridge Oriental Publications No. 35 (NY: Cambridge University Press, 1985).

76. Gerhard von Rad, *Holy War in Ancient Israel*. Trans. Marva J. Dawn, Ben C. Ollenburger, Judith E. Sanderson (Grand Rapids: Eerdmans, 1991).

77. G. Ernest Wright, *God Who Acts: Biblical Theology as Recital*. Studies in Biblical Theology No. 8 (London: SCM Press, 1966).

78. G. Ernest Wright, *The Old Testament Against its Environment*. Studies in Biblical Theology, No. 2 (London: SCM Press, 1962).

79. Davies, pp. 84-89.

80. Davies, p. 78

81. Paul D. Hanson, *The Dawn of Apocalyptic: The Historical and Sociological Roots of Jewish Apocalyptic Eschatology* (Philadelphia: Fortress Press, 1975).

82. Eliade, *The Sacred and the Profane*.

83. Gordon D. Kaufman, *Systematic Theology: A Historicist Perspective* (NY: Scribners, 1968), p. 433.

84. Margaret Barker, *The Gate of Heaven: The History and Symbolism of the Temple in Jerusalem* (London: SPCK, 1991), p. 66: "In its original setting it did not describe the events of the Exodus. The poem in fact tells the ancient story of the creation."

85. Isaiah 30:7 compares an impotent Egypt with the inert, slain monster Rahab but does not actually, as I read it, call Egypt Rahab.

86. Noth, *History of Pentateuchal Traditions*, p. 163.

87. Garbini, pp. 137-140.

88. Davies, p. 114.

Chapter Two

I Wonder as They Wander

The stories to be examined next are presented as incidents occurring during the forty years in which Israel wandered in the Sinai Desert. We must wonder, however, if the whole wandering motif reflects not the actual historical existence of Israelite nomadism, but is instead the simple result of an ancient narrative technique.

When ancient writers had before them a pile of isolated episodes, they often strung them together like pearls on a string. The pioneer form-critic Karl Ludwig Schmidt demonstrated the sheer artificiality of the sequence of events in Mark's gospel.[1] Had Jesus actually been an itinerant healer and teacher? Or was his itineracy simply a narrative gimmick for connecting the dots? Probably the latter. And the same may be the case with the tales of Moses and his people wandering the Sinai.

For this reason, I propose to dispense with the order of the desert episodes and instead to organize them by form-critical categories. Here they are.

Exodus 18:1-27; Numbers 11:11-12, 14, 16, 24-30

Establishing the Great Synagogue

These twin passages are alternate versions of a tale put about to give a Mosaic pedigree to what would in later years come to be called the Great Synagogue, or Great Assembly ("synagogue" simply being the Greek word for "coming together"). In New Testament times it (or its successor or revival) was known as the *Sanhedrin*.

Numbers 11:11-12, 14, 16, 24-30

Mosaic Pentecost

> And Moses said unto Yahweh, Wherefore hast thou dealt ill with thy servant? and wherefore have I not found favor in thy sight, that thou layest the burden of all this people upon me? Have I conceived all this people? have I brought them forth, that thou shouldest say unto me, Carry them in thy bosom, as a nursing-father carrieth the sucking child, unto the land which thou swarest unto their fathers?

> I am not able to bear all this people alone, because it is too

heavy for me.

And Yahweh said unto Moses, Gather unto me seventy men of the elders of Israel, whom thou knowest to be the elders of the people, and officers over them; and bring them unto the tent of meeting, that they may stand there with thee.

And Moses went out, and told the people the words of Yahweh: and he gathered seventy men of the elders of the people, and set them round about the Tent. And Yahweh came down in the cloud, and spake unto him, and took of the Spirit that was upon him, and put it upon the seventy elders: and it came to pass, that, when the Spirit rested upon them, they prophesied, but they did so no more. But there remained two men in the camp, the name of the one was Eldad, and the name of the other Medad: and the Spirit rested upon them; and they were of them that were written, but had not gone out unto the Tent; and they prophesied in the camp. And there ran a young man, and told Moses, and said, Eldad and Medad do prophesy in the camp. And Joshua the son of Nun, the minister of Moses, one of his chosen men, answered and said, My lord Moses, forbid them. And Moses said unto him, Art thou jealous for my sake? would that all Yahweh's people were prophets, that Yahweh would put his Spirit upon them! And Moses gat him into the camp, he and the elders of Israel. [Num. 11:11-12, 14, 16, 24-30, ASV]

There were seventy members. That, no doubt, was originally intended to reflect the heavenly council seen several times in the Bible: the assembly of the sons of God, the subordinates of El Elyon, the Most High God, whose very name marks him as the chief of deities. Each of these gods was in charge of one of the nations, which Jewish lore numbered seventy (sometimes seventy-two). Later, one of these lesser gods, Yahweh (Jehovah), patron deity of Israel (Deut. 32:8-9), was elevated to co-regent with or successor to El Elyon, his father (Dan. 7:2-14), and eventually fused together with him as if the two had always been merely different designations of the same god (Gen. 14:17-23).

More conservative-leaning scholars in the tradition of William Foxwell Albright preferred to compare the biblical Yahweh with the chief of the Canaanite pantheon, El, on the comfortable assumption that El(ohim) and Yahweh were two names for the same deity, against Otto Esisfeldt, who pointed out the implications of Deuteronomy 32:8-9. Though they readily admitted that Yahweh was in many respects strikingly parallel to El's son Baal, these scholars wanted ancient Israel, like modern Judaism, to be monotheistic, or nearly so.[2]

But as Garbini[3] notes, a Ugaritic (Canaanite) Baal text (VI AB, IV, 13-14) features El declaring, "The name of my son is Yaw." Thus, not only is the Old Testament Yahweh analogous to the Canaanite Baal, also called Yahweh/Yaw, he was originally simply the same deity, just as the Old Testament El is plainly to be identified with the Canaanite El. We can see the beginning of the Israelite attempt to differentiate their own Yahweh from his Canaanite counterpart in Hosea 2:16: "In that day, says Yahweh, you will call me 'my husband,' and no longer will you call me, 'My Baal.'"

I regard this text as precisely parallel to Exodus 6:2-3 ("I am Yahweh. I appeared to Abraham, to Isaac, to Jacob, as El Shaddai, but by my name Yahweh I did not make myself known to them.") and 3:15 ("Say this to the people of Israel, 'Yahweh, the God of your fathers, the God of Abraham, the God of Isaac, the God of Jacob, has sent me to you.' This is my name forever, and thus I am to be remembered throughout all generations"). And think of the hero Gideon, originally named Jerub-Baal (Judg. 6:32), "Let Baal contend," i.e., on his behalf, a name given to him at birth, a prayer for Baal to fight for him against misfortune all his life. It has been reinterpreted as a defiant challenge to Baal to avenge himself against Gideon if he dares, a redaction presupposing that Yahweh is no longer identified with Baal as in the old days.

Yahweh was believed to call periodic meetings of the divine council (Ps. 82:1; 89:5-7; Job:1:6; 2:1; 1 Kings 22:19-22; Isa. 6:1-8; Zech. 3:1-10) atop Mount Zaphon (mistranslated until recently as "the sides of the north" in Isa. 14:13). Just as the king of Judah (like all ancient kings) was deemed Yahweh's vicar or viceroy on earth, so was the Great Assembly the earthly counterpart of the whole divine Politburo. Thus their authority.

This went well beyond the insight of Proverbs 15:22, "Without counsel plans go wrong, but with many advisers they succeed." Rather, the idea is exactly as stated in Matthew 16:19 and 18:18: "Whatever you bind on earth shall be bound in heaven; whatever you loose on earth shall be loosed in heaven," using the ancient language of regulations and legal decisions (c.f. Matt. 23:4).

Of course, as Israelites and Jews moved from polytheism to monotheism (at least among the intelligentsia and the official hierarchy), the original notion of an earthly version of the heavenly council could not be maintained, so "the men of the Great Assembly" (*Pirke Aboth* 1:1) had to derive their authority from a different, more theologically acceptable source, namely Moses, Jehovah's mortal confidant and spokesman. That is what is happening in this passage. As often, the story is, then, re-explaining, giving a brand new legitimization for some legal arrangement when an old one no longer worked.

Mark 3:19b-21, 31-35; 13-19a is based on the first version; Mark 9:38-39 and Acts 2:1-4 are based on the second.

> Then Moses and Aaron, Nadab, and Abihu, and seventy of the elders of Israel went up, and they saw the God of Israel; and there was under his feet as it were a pavement of sapphire stone, like the very heaven for clearness. And he did not lay his hand on the chief men of the people of Israel; they beheld God, and ate and drank. [Exod. 24:9-11]

> And he said, Show me, I pray thee, thy glory. And he said, I will make all my goodness pass before thee, and will proclaim the name of Yahweh before thee; and I will be gracious to whom I will be gracious, and will show mercy on whom I will show mercy. And he said, Thou canst not see my face; for man shall not see me and live. and Yahweh said, Behold, there is a place by me, and thou shalt stand upon the rock: and it shall come to pass, while my glory passeth by, that I will put thee in a cleft of the rock, and will cover thee with my hand until I have passed by: and I will take away my hand, and thou shalt see my back; but my face shall not be seen. [Exod. 33:18-23, ASV]

Though elsewhere we read that Moses beheld Yahweh face to face, these two stories are not quite so bold.

The first story reminds us of the gospel story of the Transfiguration (Mark 9:2-8; Matt. 17:1-8; Luke 9:28-36), where Jesus ascends a mountain accompanied by a select group who see him in his previously hidden heavenly glory. One cannot help suspecting that the restriction of the actual sight of Almighty God to a group of seventy-four people is a piece of priestcraft pretending to provide assurance that there is a God, that people have indeed seen him with their own eyes—and that that's going to have to be enough for you.

I guess you just had to be there. It is precisely the same case with the resurrection narratives. You don't just have to have faith that Jesus rose from the dead. People saw him! And how do you know they saw him? Well, you're just going to have to believe they did.

The story also serves as something of a cameo of the sequence where Moses sees the heavenly Tabernacle and is instructed to reproduce it exactly in crude matter on the earth below (Exod. 25:9). Here Moses and his comrades see not only God (part of him, anyway) but the sapphire pavement of the heavenly firmament above which he dwells. It is, of course, the blue of the (solid) sky.

Do we find a contradiction to the notion that mortals cannot survive the sight of God? No. Moses, the priests, and the elders see only the feet of God standing upon the firmament.[4] The Exodus 32 story makes the Medusa-like danger of seeing God's face explicit. That is why Moses is permitted to behold only God's broad back as he recedes.

Noth suggests that, before the addition of Moses and Aaron, the priests Nadab and Abihu (soon doomed to flaming death for getting the incense recipe wrong, Lev. 10:1ff) were the stars of the story. Nadab and Abihu must have been the eponymous ancestors/founders of two priestly subgroups. This Exodus story added them to the mountaintop party to enhance their position. This priestly encounter with God on the very verge of heaven, atop the cosmic mountain, was represented in the temple service by the entry of the high priest into the Holy of Holies, the earthly copy of (and portal to) the heavenly throne room. We must understand the story of Nadab and Abihu in the larger trajectory of priestly apocalyptic visions of heaven,[5] as in Ezekiel's vision of the heavenly temple (Ezekiel 40-43) and the Testament of Levi.

But how the mighty are fallen! Leviticus chooses them for its cautionary tale because eventually their orders petered out or were eliminated.

And before Nadab and Abihu, it was simply the anonymous elders of Israel who got a glimpse of God.[6]

Exodus 32:2-4a, 24, 4c-5
Origin of the Golden Calf

The story of the manufacture of the Golden Calf idol is one of the most intricate redactional puzzles that meets us in Exodus, and yet it is by no means baffling. In its final, canonical form it is the sad story of Israel's religious declension, sometimes understood as apostasy from Yahweh, sometimes as a slightly less serious offense, the abandonment of "aniconic" worship, i.e., fashioning no earthly image of Yahweh himself or any of his celestial assistants (Exod. 20: 4; 34:17). God and Moses get pretty mad at these developments–even though, at this point in the story, the people have never been commanded not to make images.

> And when the people saw that Moses delayed to come down from the mount, the people gathered themselves together unto Aaron, and said unto him, Up, make us gods, which shall go before us; for as for this Moses, the man that brought us up out of the land of Egypt, we know not what is become of him. And Aaron said unto them, Break off the golden rings, which are in the ears of your wives, of your sons, and of your daughters, and bring them unto me. And all the people brake off the golden rings which were in their ears, and brought them unto Aaron. And he received it at their hand, and fashioned it with a graving tool, and made it a molten calf: and they said, These are thy gods, O Israel, which brought thee up out of the land of Egypt. And when Aaron saw this, he built an altar before it; and Aaron made proclamation, and said, Tomorrow shall be a feast to Yahweh. [Exod. 32:1-4, ASV]

Why an image of a golden calf? To most readers, the immediate association is with a baby cow, or at best Elmer's Glue. But in fact the image was very common in the ancient Near East (many specimens have been unearthed), where the association was that of a young bull, powerful and snorting! A fitting image for a god.[7] The Canaanite El was called "Bull EL." So there is nothing incongruous in Aaron (or Jeroboam) causing a golden "calf" image to be fashioned.

If Aaron's summons to venerate the calf rings a familiar bell, it should. Aaron is made to quote the words of the Northern king Jeroboam, who, declaring independence of Davidic Judah in the south, built great Yahweh temples at the already holy cities of Dan and Bethel to forestall his subjects getting nostalgic for Solomon's temple and making pilgrimage to Jerusalem.

> And Jeroboam said in his heart, Now will the kingdom return to the house of David: if this people go up to offer sacrifices in the house of Yahweh at Jerusalem, then will the heart of this people turn again unto their lord, even unto Rehoboam king of Judah; and they will kill me, and return to Rehoboam king of Judah. Whereupon the king took counsel, and made two calves of gold; and he said unto them, It is too much for you to go up to Jerusalem: behold thy gods, O Israel, which brought thee up out of the land of Egypt. And he set the one in Beth-el, and the other put

he in Dan. [1 Kings 12:26-29, ASV]

He says the same thing: "O Israel, behold your God who brought you out of Egypt!" The pronoun makes it a reference to "gods" (though in itself, "Elohim" can mean either one), and this looks like a scribal change to make Jeroboam and Aaron proponents of polytheism. It seems more likely that the people are to revere the calf as an image of Yahweh who freed them from Egypt, not some other, alien deities. Likewise, what would be the point of adding other deities to Yahweh, merely diluting his glory by redistributing it to his cronies? No, the point seems to have been to represent Yahweh, the God of the exodus, in bovine form.

It begins to look like the story of Aaron unveiling the Golden Calf was originally not a sad account of apostasy and idolatry but rather one of our ceremonial myths, one repeated by the priests of Dan and Bethel when pilgrims inquired, "But how do we know this is what Yahweh really looks like?" But this suggestion, which I find quite compelling, only makes sense once we untangle the rewriting that has affected the hypothetical original.

In the story as we now read it, Moses returns during the celebration of the new image and demands to know how Aaron allowed himself to be made part of such a scheme. Embarrassed and ashamed, Aaron tries to evade responsibility in what we are intended to view as a pathetic and transparent excuse. "And I said unto them, Whosoever hath any gold, let them break it off: so they gave it me; and I cast it into the fire, and there [. . .uh,] came out this calf" (Exod. 32:24).

Why, poor Aaron did not make the idol! He merely had the people dump their gold into the furnace, and, presto! It came out spontaneously in the shape of a calf! *Riiight*. But in the original version, that of the ceremonial legend, this must be what actually happened! Behind the parody we can still detect the ancient mytheme of the divine shrine "not made with hands" (Mark 14:58; Acts 7:48; 2 Cor. 5:1; Heb. 9:11). The pilgrims to Dan and Bethel would be told that, naturally, God being invisible to mortal eyes, one must leave it up to him to choose a form under which to be represented. The only way to learn his preference was to melt the gold and let God shape it into whatever form he chose. And he did: the virile calf.

The Exodus compiler had to decide what to do with this story that he could no longer endorse, having embraced the aniconic doctrine: no images of God. And yet it was sacred tradition! Some in his community would object to its omission.[8] So he cleverly refashioned the story so he could include it by turning it against its original intent.

But that's not all: the story, thus turned on its head, came in quite handy to solve another problem. Have you ever puzzled over the inclusion in Exodus, fourteen chapters apart, two sets of Ten Commandments? In fact, it is the less familiar set in chapter 34 that is actually dubbed "the ten commandments" (Exod. 34:28, "And he wrote upon the tables the words of the covenant, the ten commandments").

Let us linger here for a moment, to sort a few things out. For one thing, as Garbini [9] points out, the depiction of Moses easily carrying the two tablets implies that the writer was thinking of small terra cotta tablets used in Babylon, which therefore must have been the place the stories originated. For another, each commandment had to have been terse and succinct, as a few still are, the longer ones having attracted scribal embellishment, the beginning of the process that would eventually issue in the Mishnah and the Gemara.

In chapter 20, Moses receives these commandments:

1. You shall have no other gods before (or beside) me.

Israel (actually, Jews of a later era) are to practice monolatry, the worship of one god. This did not imply there were no other gods. The difference between monotheism and monolatry is that the former posits the existence of only one deity, all others being false figments. Isaiah 44:6 (written late in the Babylonian Exile) is a forthright affirmation of monotheism: "Thus says Yahweh, the King of Israel and his Redeemer, Yahweh Sabaoth: 'I am the first and I am the last; besides me there is no god!'" Monolatry, by contrast, takes for granted the existence of other deities but forbids their worship.

Elijah did not mind that Philistines worshipped Baal, but he was jealous for Yahweh, the one husband of Israel. Israelites had no business worshipping an alien god. After all, it was Yahweh, not Baal or Thoth or Dagon, who rescued the children of Israel from slavery to Pharaoh. They owed him a debt of gratitude, hence worship, no one else. Presumably monolatry evolved into monotheism, or at least was replaced by it. But it is impossible to use these texts to trace the progression. Exodus 20's commandments may be older than the oracle in Isaiah 44, even though the two texts as we have them were probably not written many decades apart. The thing is, older beliefs linger and coexist with newer ones for shorter or longer periods. Not everyone believed the same thing at the same time.

2. You shall not make for yourself a graven image.

Of what? Of God or any of his heavenly attendants, but this is inference, and such extrapolations were added as glosses to clarify and specify the commandment. Here is the aniconic theology.

3. You shall not take the name of Yahweh your God in vain.

Sanctions are added, but this was but the beginning of attempts to elaborate and elucidate the commandment. All right, one must take care not to misuse the divine name. But what would constitute misuse? It seems certain that the intention was to ban perjury (though that is also touched on in the ninth commandment). And breach of contract. The witness on the stand was put on oath with the formula "Give glory to Yahweh, God of Israel, and render praise to him; and tell me now what you have done. Do not hide it from me." (Josh. 7:19). He would then swear he was telling the truth, "As Yahweh lives [1 Sam. 19:6; Jer. 12:16; 23:7-8, etc.], I did not steal Melchizedek's lawn-mower!" Nothing is more true than that Yahweh lives, right? What the witness says, he wants us to believe, is equally true. He is taking, i.e., invoking, the name of Yahweh, and he will be in big trouble if he fibs. That would be taking his name in vain, emptily, as there is no truth behind it.

If I am a builder and I contract with you to have a job finished by so-and-so date and at such-and such amount, I will seal the deal by an oath in Yahweh's name, invoking him to keep accounts and to punish me if I fail to live up to the terms of our agreement. Laban says as much to his son-in-law Jacob, whom he has given little cause to trust him: "May Yahweh watch between you and me, when we are absent one from the other. If you ill-treat my daughters, or if you take wives besides my daughters, although no man is with us [to report it to me], remember, God is witness between you and me" (Gen. 31:49-50). The main job of the Persian god Mithras was to watch over and enforce pacts. Same idea. So if I fail to hold up my end of the bargain, I will have taken the name of Yahweh in vain, and God will get me.

Blasphemy involving the sacred name was a stoning offense: "Whoever curses his God shall bear his sin. He who blasphemes the name of Yahweh shall be put to death; all the congregation shall stone him" (Lev. 24:15-16). At some point the usage of the divine name was severely curtailed. It seems that the word *nachav*, rendered "blasphemes" just above, sometimes means "to pronounce distinctly." This would mean that simply saying "Yahweh" would be a capital offense! The Greek Septuagint translation as well as the Aramaic paraphrase Targum Onkelos both render it this way, so it became a common reading. Even in the synagogue liturgy, when the lay reader came to the name "Yahweh," a mark in the text reminded him not to say it aloud, but to substitute for it "Adonai" (cf. the Syrian god Adonis), another biblical divine name that for some reason did not carry the same danger.[10]

But eventually it got to the point we see in Monty Python's *The Life of Brian*, where poor old Matthias, son of Deuteronomy of Gath, is about to be stoned and protests, "Look, I'd had a lovely supper and all I said to my wife was, 'That piece of halibut was good enough for Jehovah.'" [11] That's right: The scribes ruled that no one should ever take the name of Yahweh on his lips–with one exception: the high priest might (indeed must) utter it once a year on the Day of Atonement. But Simon the Just (300-270 BCE) was reportedly the last to be allowed to do even this. Here we have a (or even *the*) classic case of "building a hedge about the Torah," erecting a protective screen of "extra mile" rules around the basic commandments so no one would easily get within breaking distance of them!

4. Remember to keep the Sabbath day holy.

Verses 9-10 ("Six days you shall labor and do all your work, but the seventh day is a Sabbath to Yahweh your God. In it you shall not do any work, you or your son or your daughter, your manservant or your maidservant or your cattle or the sojourner who is within your gates.") have been tacked on by the Deuteronomic redactor, as they bear Deuteronomy's hallmarks of humanitarian concern for children, slaves, animals and resident foreigners. Verse 11 ("For in six days Yahweh made heaven and earth, the sea, and all that is in them, and rested the seventh day; therefore Yahweh blessed the sabbath day and hallowed it."), on the other hand, is copied right out of Genesis 2:1-3, the conclusion of the Priestly creation account. The Deuteronomic and Priestly reasons for the holiness of the Sabbath are quite different though by no means incompatible.

5. Honor your father and your mother.

Again, there are added specifications, but not many.

6. You shall not commit murder.

This commandment struck no one as requiring any explanation, though modern readers require to be told that the word used here (*rasah*) is often employed in Old Testament contexts implying the unjust destruction of innocent life, not killing on the battlefield or the execution of criminals.[12]

7. You shall not commit adultery.

Apparently, men visiting prostitutes did not count as adultery, though prostitutes were adulteresses if they were also wives. Polygyny (a man as husband to more than one wife) was not adultery either. There was no Israelite polyandry (one woman married to several husbands).

8. You shall not steal.

9. You shall not bear false witness against your neighbor.

10. You shall not covet anything belonging to your neighbor.

As people tried to weasel out of this commandment, seeking convenient exceptions, scribes had to stipulate all the "things" that were off limits.

———

This list is often called "the Moral Decalogue," as behavior is the major (though not exclusive) focus.[13] The other set, in Exodus 34:14-26, is called "the Ritual Decalogue" for obvious reasons. If the Exodus 20 commandments have attracted a few cumbersome barnacles, the ones in chapter 34 are barely discernible for the thick foliage that has grown up around them.

Let's just clear away the weeds:

1. You shall worship no other god.
verse 14

2. You shall make for yourselves no molten gods.
verse 17

3. The Feast of Unleavened Bread you shall keep.
verse 18

4. All that opens the womb is mine.
verse 19

5. Six days you shall work, and on the seventh you shall rest.
verse 21

6. You shall observe the Feast of Weeks, the First Fruits of Wheat Harvest, and the Feast of Ingathering at the turn

of the year.
verse 22

7. You shall not offer the blood of my sacrifice with leaven.
verse 25

8. Neither shall the sacrifice of the Feast of the Passover be left until the morning.
verse 25

9. The first fruits of your ground you shall bring to the house of Yahweh your God.
verse 26

10. You shall not boil a kid in its mother's milk.
verse 26

———

There is no persuasive explanation for that climactic tenth commandment. At least few people are tempted to break it! It has grown into the fundamental kosher law that Jews must not consume meat and milk together.

Back to the Golden Calf debacle: The compiler put his rewritten version of the story to good use. He had two different lists of commandments that overlapped only at three points. Presumably each list of "top ten commandments" had its powerful partisans, just as each of the Genesis Flood stories (from J and P) did.

The Genesis compiler could not very well simply place the two Noah stories side by side since each concludes with God promising never again to destroy mankind. A simple juxtaposition would make it look as if God turns on the hose right after swearing not to flood his creatures. So the only option was to razor the stories into confetti, then splice them together, even though this procedure resulted in stubborn contradictions, not to mention verbose redundancy. The Priestly author was already windy and pedantic enough by himself!

Here with the two sets of commandments, however, one might use both lists separately. Indeed one must. His expedient was to use the outrage of the Golden Calf as a transition between the sets. Moses hit the ceiling when he saw the idol and in his disgust decided these people were unworthy of the laws of God. Unwilling to cast his pearls before swine, he dashed the inscribed terra cotta plaques to the ground. A little while later God called him back up the mountain to provide him with a new "copy." Only it is anything but a copy.

As we have seen, there are only three matching commandments. It was the best he could do, a compromise document. And it was a pretty good attempt, all things considered. Ultimately, what's the difference? There are a total of five hundred ninety other Torah commandments anyway, not just ten.

Exodus 32:25-29

Origin of the Levites

The Levite priesthood originally must have served as "those skilled to rouse up Leviathan" (Job 3:8),[14] priests of the serpent (dragon) god *Nehushtan*, who, as per 2 Kings 18:1-4, was offered sacrifices of incense. "Nehushtan" comes from the Hebrew *nahash*, and "Leviathan" is derived from *levi*, both of which mean "serpent," plus the honorific suffix.[15] He was a deity with his own worshippers, as we can see from the occurrence in the Bible of theophoric names containing his—equivalents to names like Ananias or Hananiyah "gift of Yahweh") and Elhanan ("gift of El"). Nehushtan names attested in the Bible are Nahash, king of Ammon (1 Sam. 11:1. etc.), and Naashon (Exod. 6:23). Leviathan/Nehushtan was apparently also called Rahab (Pss. 89:10; Isa. 51:9), and the Jericho harlot Rahab (Josh 2:1, etc.) was most likely a sacred prostitute (I like to call them "priestitutes") who served the temple of the dragon god.[16]

Dare we ask if the nonconformist *Rechab*ites might have been Rahab worshippers? Margaret Barker[17] sees them as refugees fleeing Jerusalem in order to keep their pre-Deuteronomic traditions. Could Rahab-worship have been one of them? And could Rehoboth and Beth-Rehob (2 Sam. 10:5) have been named for the presence of Rahab cult centers there, just as Jeremiah's home town Anathoth was named for the worship of Anath predominant there? [18] Might Rehabiah (1 Chron. 23:17), ben-Rehob (2 Sam. 10:5), and even Rehoboam (which T.K. Cheyne corrected to "Rehab-el") [19] have been theophoric personal names from this tradition?

The stories of Yahweh's victories over Leviathan/Rahab seem to enshrine the ascendancy of Yahweh's cult over that of his ophidian rival, an aftershock of which can be felt in 2 Kings 18:1-5, where Yahwist King Hezekiah has Nehushtan's effigy put out to the curb.

Now it came to pass in the third year of Hoshea son of Elah king of
Israel, that Hezekiah the son of Ahaz king of Judah began to reign.
Twenty and five years old was he when he began to reign; and he
reigned twenty and nine years in Jerusalem: and his mother's
name was Abi the daughter of Zechariah. And he did that which
was right in the eyes of Yahweh, according to all that David his
father had done. He removed the high places, and brake the
pillars, and cut down the Asherah: and he brake in pieces the
brazen serpent that Moses had made; for unto those days the
children of Israel did burn incense to it; and he called it
Nehushtan. He trusted in Yahweh, the God of Israel; so that after
him was none like him among all the kings of Judah, nor among
them that were before him. [ASV]

Up till this point, Nehushtan/Leviathan must have retained a subordinate
place in the Yahwist pantheon, and the Levites served him. But with their
patron deity's expulsion, the Levite order was demoted (Ezek, 44:9-14) to
the status of sacred functionaries: doorkeepers, singers and composers,
etc., which meant they were no longer paid in sacrificial meat, no longer
being sacrificial officiants. We will read of a labor dispute between one of
the Levitical guilds of choristers (the house of Korah) and the Aaronide
priests over precisely this issue. But for the moment let us note the lasting
monument of the Levite servitors of Nehushtan. This is the Hebrew
counterpart to the Greek myth of the Titan Prometheus.[20]

Prometheus, Zeus' cousin, was a surviving member of the previous
divine regime, his presence tolerated on Olympus in the same way King
David retained Meribaal ("Mephibosheth"),[21] the last member of his
predecessor Saul's house, in his own court (2 Sam. chapter 9). Zeus had
created humanity but was not much interested in their welfare. Prometheus
took an interest in them and decided to act on their behalf. First, he tricked
Zeus into choosing the fat and entrails of sacrificial animals as his portion,
leaving the choice cuts of meat to the hungry mortals. Then he contrived to
smuggle fire from heaven and to bring it to the shivering cave men on earth
below.

For this effrontery Zeus sentenced him to be crucified to a boulder,
where he must endure the daily visits of a vulture to eat his ever-
regenerating liver. It is Prometheus who is the hero and benefactor of
mankind, not Zeus the creator. But he had been displaced by the stronger
cult of Zeus, and that could not be gainsaid. So the story laments the fall of
the story-teller's god: "Right forever on the gallows; wrong forever

on the throne."

We ought to recognize the same point being made in the Garden of Eden story. Yahweh has created mankind but is in no hurry to share his prerogatives with the man and the woman. Most of all, he wanted to prevent their learning the secret of procreation, a privilege exclusive to Yahweh and the sons of El. He had need of but a single caretaker for his pleasure garden and provided a companion only as an afterthought to mitigate the man's loneliness, since the animals, initially created for that purpose, were inadequate to the task, presumably because they could not speak. The man and the woman might eat of the Tree of Life (though we later learn they had not gotten around to it) because Yahweh wanted them to continue on and on in their duties, with no need of replacement. We must assume that Yahweh and his fellow deities renewed their own immortality the same way, just as the Olympian gods gained nourishment from nectar and ambrosia (as well as sacrificial smoke–cf. Gen. 8:20-21). What he did not want was for them to eat the fruit of the Tree of Knowledge, which at least included carnal knowledge: the ability to reproduce.

Remember, two were enough. If the man and the woman were to gain divine knowledge and the ability to reproduce indefinitely, why then, the world should be full of competing gods! To keep their hands off the merchandise, Yahweh tells them that the Tree's fruit is poisonous (at least to humans), and if they take so much as a bite, it will kill them instantly!

The Serpent, however, acts as the welcoming committee, striking up a conversation with the woman, in the course of which she tells him of Yahweh's warning. The Serpent advises her that Yahweh is lying in order to keep them from his special stash. He wants to keep them in ignorance, which a bite of the fruit will remedy. She realizes it is not poison ("seeing that it was good for food") but is desirable for the knowledge it will convey, so she and her husband, silently observing up to this point, hasten to avail themselves of it.

They have sex, the forbidden fruit, which is why, once Yahweh discovers their disobedience, he makes the punishment fit the crime. The horse has escaped the barn; she can and will have children, even as Yahweh and the gods do, but he will make her rue this day. Childbirth will be full of pain, and she will curse her husband every time. So the earth will eventually be filled with pesky humans who may one day challenge the gods themselves (Gen. 11:5-7). But how much worse it would be if all the humans should be immortal to boot! Hence Yahweh's urgent appeal to his fellows to expel the man and the woman from Eden before they get a chance to sample the Tree of Life!

And the Serpent's fate? He and his progeny will be demoted to crawling on the ground, whereas previously he had (presumably) flown with wings (Isa. 6:2). Henceforth, snakes and humans will be bitter enemies so that they may never ally against Yahweh again. Humans will bash snakes' brains in with garden hoes and shoot their pistols at rattlers.

But was the Serpent a villain? No, worse than that: He was the loser. The benefactor of humankind, this earned him the Creator's scorn, just as Prometheus' pity for humans had prompted Zeus' vengeance. Yahweh was the liar, not the serpent. Who was the champion of humans? Not God. Not the God Yahweh. Rather, Nehushtan. Who would have told such a story? Isn't it obvious? It must have been one of the Levites. He could not deny that Yahweh had become king of the holy hill, that Nehushtan had lost out. But Nehushtan's priest would get his licks in and make sure the truth of his god survived for any who could read and understand it.[22]

Once the god Nehushtan had been exorcised from Jewish worship, the demoted Levite priesthood had to be given a new, orthodox pedigree. In fact, there are three of them. Since such a foundation legend for a guild is considered very sacred by the members, no one can get away with dropping it, even if there are rival versions that do not agree! And, of course, the very fact of competing versions means that no one knew (or liked) the real origin. Judges (17:7-13; 18:1-31) portrays the Levites as local or itinerant oracle-mongers who told fortunes much in the fashion of the shaman-like *nabi* prophets like Samuel (1 Sam. 9:6-9). The name Levite here denotes a profession, equivalent to the Hebrew *kohen* (cf. Arabic *kahin*,[23] pre-Islamic oracle-mongers), and most definitely not a tribe, for the Levite in this story is explicitly said to belong to the tribe of Judah (Judg. 17:7).

This fits well with the fact that elsewhere we find lists of the tribes of Israel that do not even include Levi as a tribe. Some lists do not even have twelve of them (Josh. chapter 1; Judg. 5:1-18), and in these a tribe of Levi is conspicuous by its absence.[24] It is possible that some Levites, cut loose from the Yahwist establishment with the ouster of the Nehushtan cult, made what living they could as household priests and itinerant fortune-tellers, continuing one of their main functions.

Oracle-mongering was still connected with serpent deities in the second century CE, as we read in Lucian of Samosata's satire *Alexander the False Prophet*. Alexander of Abonutichus, a clever rogue, tricked out a large snake with a linen mask with human features, complete with puppet strings he could pull to manipulate the god's mouth. He called it Glycon and charged admission to his circus tent to see it. Suppliants lined up with questions written on paper notes, handed to the priests, and Alexander would write answers and hand them back from concealment.[25] (Not unlike Madame Blavatsky, with her revelations from the Ascended Masters, conveniently written on folded slips of paper dropped through ceiling vents.)

This Exodus version understands the Levites along the lines of the Mormon Danites: armed and pitiless enforcers of Yahwistic orthodoxy.

> And when Moses saw that the people were broken loose, (for Aaron had let them loose for a derision among their enemies,) then Moses stood in the gate of the camp, and said, Whoso is on Yahweh's side, let him come unto me. And all the sons of Levi gathered themselves together unto him. And he said unto them, Thus saith Yahweh, the God of Israel, Put ye every man his sword upon his thigh, and go to and fro from gate to gate throughout the camp, and slay every man his brother, and every man his companion, and every man his neighbor. And the sons of Levi did according to the word of Moses: and there fell of the people that day about three thousand men. And Moses said, Consecrate yourselves to-day to Yahweh, yea, every man against his son, and against his brother; that he may bestow upon you a blessing this day. [Exod. 32:25-29, ASV]

At first it seemed that all the children of Israel had joined in the idolatrous orgy, but now it appears that Yahweh had kept back for himself a remnant (cf. 1 Kings 19:18) in order to slay the apostates and thus to purify the community from idolaters. In any case, their fanatical zeal for Yahweh has proven their worth and established their and their descendants' place as priestly servitors of Yahweh. This account would seem to be the product of Levites "protesting too much" their loyalty to the Yahweh cult which had shut down their own ancestral Nehushtan worship.

If so much of the Old Testament history is fictive and legendary, we have to ask, "Was there ever really a Josianic reform?" That may be beside the point. I think of the standardization of the text of the Koran by the Caliph Uthman. We read that theological disputes could not be resolved as long as one party cited Koranic verses absent from his opponent's copy. Today, of course, such differences of opinion would be settled via letter bombs, but

Uthman's solution was to call in all copies of the sacred text and to set textual critics to work creating a *textus receptus*. He then burned all the old copies and replaced them with the "Revised Standard Version."

Yet recent critical scholarship on Islamic origins (pretty late in coming!) suggests that there was never such an Uthmanic standardization.[26] (There are similar doubts as to whether the Rabbinical confab at Yavneh/Jamnia ever happened, but that's yet another story!) The story seems rather to have been made up by clever Muslim savants who wanted, so to speak, to induct their pet opinions retroactively into the holy text. They would fabricate some "Koranic" verse and claim that it had been present in a copy treasured by their family and never turned in to Uthman's censors. The implication was that "It ain't in the Bible, but it oughta be!"

One must wonder if Jewish scribes did not posit a Josianic "reformation" in order to claim that their own beliefs, frowned on by the authorities in their day, were actually older than the roots of contemporary orthodoxy, whether they were or not. This may denote that, like various Christian Gnostic groups who fathered (or grandfathered) their own innovations on Jesus via the claim that he had taught these secrets only to a select, inner group of elite disciples, and that they had come to light only recently. But the fabrication of a Josianic reform might just as easily be a simple retrojection (for pedigree's sake) of a later suppression of ancient ideas judged incompatible with an establishment agenda.

We can already recognize in 2 Kings 18:1-4 a pushing back of the Josianic reform (2 Kings 23:1-25) into the reign of Hezekiah. Wellhausen long ago showed how the Deuteronomistic reforms were read back into Mosaic times, and then the Priestly innovations were retrojected onto Moses. Perhaps the "Josianic" reforms actually took place in the time of the "Second" Temple. The vaunted (and bemoaned) differences between the (fictive) Solomonic temple and its post- Exilic successor were really a depiction of the differences between the temple of Zerubbabel and that essentially rebuilt by Herod the Great.

The third version of Levite origins is, of course, to posit that the Levites constituted a separate sub-ethnicity, one of the tribes of Israel descended from a common father, the Patriarch Jacob. Levi presents a particularly clear case of the artificiality of the whole twelve-tribe concept.

New Origin for the Bronze Serpent

Remember how the Exodus compiler had to transform the Golden Calf if he was to use the old story at all? We see something quite similar in the case of the Bronze Serpent in the Book of Numbers. In 2 Kings 18:4 we read that Moses had caused the image of the Nehushtan to be made, which means that the nature of the relic had already been reinterpreted by Hezekiah's time. Here is that story.

> And they journeyed from mount Hor by the way to the Red Sea, to compass the land of Edom: and the soul of the people was much discouraged because of the way. And the people spake against God, and against Moses, Wherefore have ye brought us up out of Egypt to die in the wilderness? for there is no bread, and there is no water; and our soul loatheth this light bread. And Yahweh sent fiery serpents among the people, and they bit the people; and much people of Israel died. And the people came to Moses, and said, We have sinned, because we have spoken against Yahweh, and against thee; pray unto Yahweh, that he take away the serpents from us. And Moses prayed for the people. And Yahweh said unto Moses, Make thee a fiery serpent, and set it upon a standard: and it shall come to pass, that every one that is bitten, when he seeth it, shall live. And Moses made a serpent of brass, and set it upon the standard: and it came to pass, that if a serpent had bitten any man, when he looked unto the serpent of brass, he lived. [Num. 21:4-9, ASV]

Now there is no reference to Nehushtan in sight. This new ceremonial myth reinterprets the bronze effigy of that deity as an apotropaic ("turning away") device, a piece of imitative magic. Moses cures poisonous snakebites by hoisting aloft a bronze image of one of the serpents. There is still a vestigial hint of the original significance in that the term seraphim ("burning ones") in this context denotes the burning pain from the poison.

In Isaiah 6, however, we read of fiery, winged beings flanking the throne of Yahweh. We saw that the Edenic Serpent, a reflection of the god Nehushtan, had possessed some other mode of locomotion before Yahweh grounded him, and that this might have been flight. It is tempting to suggest that Nehushtan had been the patron and prototype of the fiery serpents. But all this is visible, if at all, only between the lines of Numbers 21:4-9. By the time of Hezekiah's Puritan smashing of the Bronze Serpent, the object was understood as a relic of Moses in the wilderness, one venerated rather too much by pilgrims who offered incense to it. But the old name Nehushtan could not be suppressed and had not been forgotten.

One last note: obviously, the Bronze Serpent as depicted here is identical to the Caduceus of Apollo, who was a healer and a sun god. (He traded it to Hermes, which is why we now usually associate it with the messenger god.) We will see that Moses, too, began as a law-giving sun god.

War-Chant of the Bearers of the Ark of the Covenant

Numbers 10:33-36 offers a shorter version of a psalm sung by the Levitical bearers of the Ark of the Covenant when moved for special occasions:

> And they set forward from the mount of Yahweh three days' journey; and the ark of the covenant of Yahweh went before them three days' journey, to seek out a resting-place for them. And the cloud of Yahweh was over them by day, when they set forward from the camp. And it came to pass, when the ark set forward, that Moses said, Rise up, O Yahweh, and let thine enemies be scattered; and let them that hate thee flee before thee. And when it rested, he said, Return, O Yahweh, unto the ten thousands of the thousands of Israel. [ASV]

And here is the longer version, formatted lyrically:

> Let God arise, let his enemies be scattered;
>   let those who hate him flee before him!
> As smoke is driven away, so drive them away;
>   as wax melts before fire,
>   let the wicked perish before God!
> But let the righteous be joyful;
>   let them exult before God;
>   let them be jubilant with joy!
>
> Sing to God, sing praises to his name;
>   lift up a song to him who rides upon the clouds;
>   his name is the LORD [Yahweh], exult before him!
>
> Father of the fatherless and protector of widows
>   is God in his holy habitation.
> God gives the desolate a home to dwell in;
>   he leads out the prisoners to prosperity;
>   but the rebellious dwell in a parched land.

God, when thou didst go forth before thy people,
when thou didst march through the wilderness, Selah.
the earth quaked, the heavens poured down rain,
at the presence of God;
yon Sinai quaked at the presence of God,
the God of Israel.
Rain in abundance, O God, thou didst shed abroad;
thou didst restore thy heritage as it languished;
thy flock found a dwelling in it;
in thy goodness, O God, thou didst provide for the needy.

The LORD [Yahweh] gives the command;
great is the host of those who bore the tidings:
"The kings of the armies, they flee, they flee!"
The women at home divide the spoil,
though they stay among the sheepfolds—
the wings of a dove covered with silver,
its pinions with green gold.
When the Almighty scattered kings there,
snow fell on Zalmon.

O mighty mountain, mountain of Bashan;
O many-peaked mountain, mountain of Bashan!
Why look you with envy, O many-peaked mountain,
at the mount which God desired for his abode,
yea, where the LORD [Yahweh] will dwell for ever?

With mighty chariotry, twice ten thousand,
thousands upon thousands,
the Lord [Adonai] came from Sinai into the holy place.
Thou didst ascend the high mount,
leading captives in thy train,
and receiving gifts among men,
even among the rebellious, that the LORD [Yahweh] God may
dwell there.

Blessed be the Lord [Adonai],
who daily bears us up;
God is our salvation. Selah.
Our God is a God of salvation;
and to GOD [Yahweh], the Lord [Adonai], belongs escape
from death.

But God will shatter the heads of his enemies,
the hairy crown of him who walks in his guilty ways.

The Lord [Adonai] said,
"I will bring them back from Bashan,
I will bring them back from the depths of the sea,
that you may bathe your feet in blood,
that the tongues of your dogs may have their portion
     from the foe."

The chant implies that the Ark was being carried onto the battlefield as Israel's "secret weapon." It was the portable throne of Yahweh, who sat invisibly enthroned atop it, attended by effigies of the mythological cherubs (probably depicted as winged lions with human faces), which were personifications of the clouds that drew his sky chariot. It was essentially imitative magic, pantomiming the advance of the warrior storm god to the field of battle through the thundering skies.

There is a wonderful faux Doré engraving on display in an early scene of *Raiders of the Lost Ark* in which death rays are seen projecting from the Ark of the Covenant, incinerating heathen troops. That goes a bit farther than anything the Bible says, but it does prompt us to ask what help the ancients imagined the presence of the Ark to offer. Just a good luck charm?

Joshua 6 has the Ark carried by Levites, like a coffin by pall-bearers, around the walled circumference of Jericho. Accompanied by apocalyptic trumpet blasts and war shouts from the troops, the Ark's presence caused the vainly fortified walls to topple. Pretty impressive; too bad it didn't happen.

In what looks at first to be a more modest account of the Ark on the battlefield (1 Samuel chapters 4-6), the Ark seems to be of little help. The Philistines defeat the Israelite troops, and the Ark itself is captured and displayed as a war trophy by the Philistines. But it soon becomes clear that what we have here is really something of an Israelite version of the Trojan Horse.

The Philistines begin to suffer plagues of mice infestation and Bubonic Plague! They try to turn back the disasters with the same sort of apotropaic magic Moses used with the Bronze Serpent: they fashion gold replicas of the mice and the tumors, hoping the real things will disappear. This doesn't help, so they begin to surmise that it has something to do with the captured Ark. Perhaps the god to whom it rightly belongs is applying heavy sanctions to force the Philistines to cough up his Ark.

To test the hypothesis, they place the Ark on the flatbed of a brand-new oxcart drawn by brand new oxen (only the best for a deity, which is also why Jesus must be buried in a brand-new tomb in Luke 23:53). They prod the beasts to get moving but do not aim them in any direction. If they are right, the animals will make a bee-line for the Israelite border, signifying that Yahweh is invisibly at the reins. And so it happens. In short, God smuggled himself behind the lines by allowing the uncircumcised heathen to capture him (in or on his Ark), and there he wreaked far more havoc than he would have on the battlefield.

Did the Levite priests ever pick up the Ark and carry it places? There might have been such a portable shrine in ancient times; we know of others. But I suspect that, once deposited in the temple (if it ever even was!), it was there for the long haul. If it was ever taken out for public view, as the Ethiopian churches periodically bring out their versions of the Ark for ritual public display on holy days, perhaps this chant was sung. But the implied sagas of the Ark as a secret weapon on the battlefield are just that: legendary sagas.

Ethiopian church legends have Menelik I (Solomon's son with the Queen of Sheba) asking permission to make a replica of the Ark of the Covenant to take home with him, then pulling the old switcheroo, with the result that the one and only Ark now resides in Ethiopia.[27] Of course, this is an etiological legend, like that of the bogus Shroud of Turin. And I am suggesting the same was already true of the war chant of the Ark of the Covenant. Whatever Ark was ever displayed in Jewish worship was exactly like the one paraded in Ethiopian churches today: a replica of something that never existed in the first place, any more than the Trojan Horse did.

Daughters May Inherit

We are accustomed to picture the law-giver Moses as receiving the commandments on stone slabs directly from the hand of God atop Mount Sinai, as he does twice in Exodus, in chapters 20 and 34. But Exodus 15:22-25 and 18:13-16 paint a very different picture, suggesting a gradual accumulation of case law as individual parties appeared before Moses to present their disputes and complaints.

Moses is shown positioning himself beside a babbling brook. Once given a question, he would go into an oracular trance state, and the sounds of the water would stimulate his subconscious, providing an answer. That is how we might put it, but the ancients would have said Moses was interpreting the sounds of the brook as the message of God, just as Corinthians with the gift of interpreting tongues would give the sense of an utterance in the language of the angels.

Deborah (Judg. 4:4-5), one of the "judges," heard cases and ruled on them in the same way, only it was the rustling of the palm fronds under which she sat that provided her inspiration. This was the common practice of fortune-tellers and sooth-sayers in the ancient Near East. King Ahaziah sent a servant to the shrine of the Philistine god Baal-Zebub (2 Kings 1:2) to ask for a prognosis for his recovery. "Baal-Zebub" famously means "Lord of the Flies." He bore that name because he was an oracle god. His priests would go into the trance state and hear a sound like the buzzing (*al azif*) of flies, and this they interpreted as the voices of the desert sprites (*jinn*, "genies") sharing their secrets.

The *jinn* knew the future and might be persuaded to spill the beans if the price were right. Of course, like the Oracle of Apollo at Delphi, they might phrase their predictions in safely ambiguous language, like a newspaper horoscope. And, since they were constantly ranging over the desert, they might have seen the lost keys to your camel and could tell you where to find them, as Saul hopes from Samuel in 1 Samuel 9:3-8. Now look at Numbers 27:1-11.

> Then drew near the daughters of Zelophehad, the son of Hepher, the son of Gilead, the son of Machir, the son of Manasseh, of the families of Manasseh the son of Joseph; and these are the names of his daughters: Mahlah, Noah, and Hoglah, and Milcah, and Tirzah. And they stood before Moses, and before Eleazar the priest, and before the princes and all the congregation, at the door of the tent of meeting, saying, Our father died in the wilderness, and he was not among the company of them that gathered themselves together against Yahweh in the company of Korah: but he died in his own sin; and he had no sons. Why should the name of our father be taken away from among his family, because he had no son? Give unto us a possession among the brethren of our father.

> And Moses brought their cause before Yahweh. And Yahweh spake unto Moses, saying, The daughters of Zelophehad speak right: thou shalt surely give them a possession of an inheritance among their father's brethren; and thou shalt cause the inheritance of their father to pass unto them. And thou shalt speak unto the children of Israel, saying, If a man die, and have no son, then ye shall cause his inheritance to pass unto his daughter. And if he have no daughter, then ye shall give his inheritance unto his

brethren. And if he have no brethren, then ye shall give his inheritance unto his father's brethren. And if his father have no brethren, then ye shall give his inheritance unto his kinsman that is next to him of his family, and he shall possess it: and it shall be unto the children of Israel a statute and ordinance, as Yahweh commanded Moses. [ASV]

Moses is depicted in terms of the familiar soothsayers of the day, and that is what we see in Numbers 27:1-11. When approached with a case lacking precedent, Moses consults God and provides one for future cases to follow. Presumably the division of labor suggested by Jethro in Exodus 18:21-22 amounts to delegating to the subordinate judges the cases that may be settled according to the legal precedents Moses has established. That leaves Moses himself in the role of a Supreme Court should some new type of problem arise.

Notes

1. Karl Ludwig Schmidt, "Jesus Christ." In Jaroslav Pelikan, ed., *Twentieth Century Theology in the Making. I Themes of Biblical Theology.* (Selections from the second edition of *Die Religion in Geschichte und Gegenwart*) Fontana Library, Theology and Philosophy. Trans. R.A. Wilson (London: Collins, 1969), pp. 98-99.

2. Patrick D. Miller, Jr., *The Divine Warrior in Early Israel*. Harvard Semitic Monograph Series, Volume 5. (Cambridge: Harvard University Press, 1973), pp. 73-74.

3. Garbini, p. 56

4. I'm guessing this isn't one of those passages (Exod. 4:25; Ruth 3:4, 7; Isa. 7:20) where "feet" is a euphemism for "penis."

5. Margaret Barker, *Gate of Heaven*, pp. 47, 127-128, 150-177.

6. Noth, *History of Pentateuchal Traditions*, p. 186.

7. Once, while watching *The Late Show* with David Letterman (at that time still amusing), I beheld the astonishing sight of some variety of Italian bull on display for a livestock show in New York. This thing was a massive wall of muscle! It was strangely breathtaking, and at once the propriety of using such a representation for Almighty God was driven home to me.

8. Think of the 1973 publication of *The Common Bible*, the first edition of the Revised Standard Version to include the Deuterocanonical, Apocryphal books accepted by Orthodox and Catholic Churches. It was offered as a Bible all Christians could use, even if Protestants must hold their noses at some of the contents. My friend Eugene McDermott quipped that it ought to have had blank pages at the back for a "Write Your Own Scriptures" section!

9. Garbini, pp. 104-105. Otherwise poor Moses should have needed a forklift to bring them down the mountain.

10. It is out of respect for this ancient Jewish custom that even modern English Bibles avoid using the name Yahweh/Jehovah, substituting for it "Lᴏʀᴅ" or "GOD."

11. Chapman, Cleese, Gilliam, Idle, Jones, and Palin, p. 20.

12. Johann Jakob Stamm, *The Ten Commandments in Recent Research*. Trans. Maurice Edward Andrew. Studies in Biblical Theology. Second Series 2 (London: SCM Press, 1967), pp. 98-99.

13. Naturally, if the list were completely moral in character, there would be no Constitutional problem with posting the Ten Commandments in public school classrooms, but the United States Government obviously has no business mandating that its citizens shall worship the Hebrew God and none other. Have advocates of posting this Decalogue ever actually taken the trouble to *read it*? I suspect not, as most people, when quizzed, seem unable to remember *any* of the Commandments. But ignorance is no excuse before the law, even of the Law of Moses.

14. Margaret Barker, *The Risen Lord: The Jesus of History as the Christ of Faith* (Valley Forge: Trinity Press International, 1997), p. 76.

15. Goldziher, p. 184.

16. [Bible Geek listener]

17. Margaret Barker, "What Did King Josiah Reform?" Paper presented at Brigham Young University, May 6, 2003, thinlyveiled.com/barker/josiahsreform.htm

18. Patai, *Hebrew Goddess*, p. 53.

19. T.K. Cheyne, "Rehoboam." In Cheyne and J. Sutherland Black, eds., *Encyclopaedia Biblica* (London: Macmillan, 1903), col. 4027.

20. See Robert Graves, *The Greek Myths*. Volume One (Baltimore: Penguin Books, 1960), pp. 143-145.

21. The scribes did not want even to have to speak the soiled name of Baal when this passage came up in the cycle of liturgical readings (Pss. 16:4), so they replaced it with *bosheth*, "shame."

22. We can't help wondering how long the interdicted cult of Nehushtan/ Leviathan/Rahab survived underground. Might the Gnostic sect of the Ophites ("serpent-ites") or Naassenes (the Greek language equivalent) have been their heirs? They hailed the Serpent, as did many Gnostics (see the Nag Hammadi text *The Testimony of Truth*), as the true divine revealer and vilified Yahweh as "a malicious grudger." They also identified Adam with Jesus as well as the Phrygian dying and rising god Attis (*The Naassene Hymn*).

23. H.A.R. Gibb, *Mohammedanism: An Historical Survey* (NY: New American Library/Mentor Books, 1955), pp. 36-37.

24. Garbini, Chapter 10, "The Twelve Tribes," pp. 121-126. How interesting that the Old Testament lists of twelve tribes anticipate the inconsistency and confusion of the New Testament lists (Mk. 3:16-19; Matt. 10:2-4; Luke 6:14-16; John 21:2;

Acts 1:13) of the twelve disciples of Jesus, who seem to be intended as a new set of patriarchs to govern the twelve tribes of Israel in the Millennium (Matt.19:28). The names of the disciples vary, probably reflecting the figureheads of Jewish-Christian groups or factions who receded or advanced in prominence. This mirrors the shifting of the numbers and names of the ancient tribes fictively linked to Jacob.

25. Arthur Darby Nock, *Conversion: The Old and the New in Religion from Alexander the Great to Augustine of Hippo* (NY: Oxford University Press, 1933), pp. 93-96.

26. I owe this identification to Geoffrey Tolle.

27. E. A Wallis Budge, *The Queen of Sheba & her Only Son Menyelek: Being the History of the Departure of God & His Ark of the Covenant from Jerusalem to Ethiopia, and the Establishment of the Religion of the Hebrews & the Solomonic Line of Kings in That Country. A Complete Translation of Kebra Nagast.* (Medici Society, London, 1922), p. 18.

Chapter Three
Cautionary Tales

Since the invention of the printing press, Protestants have developed the pious practice of devotional Bible reading, assuming in effect that God inspired the scriptures with the common people in mind. This assumption occasions frequent stumbles, as readers wonder what on earth God may be saying to them through endless legal and ritual stipulations. They no longer realize that much of the material, especially in a book like Leviticus, was never meant for readers like them. Leviticus is a priestly handbook, a document for experts and professionals. Lay persons might as well dip into the *Sama Veda*. We will see how not only esoteric laws, but also most of the cautionary tales, are aimed at the priests and Levites.

Leviticus 10:1-3
Offering "Strange Fire"

Modern readers find it a giant impediment to faith when they read stories like this one where the Almighty Creator, the Infinite King of the Cosmos, is so urgent that the precise incense formula be used at his altar that he blasts his priests to atoms when they momentarily get careless.

> And Nadab and Abihu, the sons of Aaron, took each of them his censer, and put fire therein, and laid incense thereon, and offered strange fire before Yahweh, which he had not commanded them. And there came forth fire from before Yahweh, and devoured them, and they died before Yahweh. Then Moses said unto Aaron, This is it that Yahweh spake, saying, I will be sanctified in them that come nigh me, and before all the people I will be glorified. And Aaron held his peace. [ASV]

Likewise, can we believe that the Absolute Spirit would be so finicky as to insist that only dugong hide be used [1] for the hangings of the Tabernacle (Exod. 26:4)? On the other hand, it comes as little surprise from the priests who dominated society and wielded the power of the God they claimed to represent against kings and commoners alike.[2] People like this can readily be imagined putting their flunkies to death for goofing up the small stuff, or at least wishing they could.

Numbers 15:32-36
Violation of the Sabbath

Apparently, a mere commandment not to work on the Sabbath was not thought sufficient. Here is a (fictive) precedent for such cases.[3] Note the intentional triviality of the case. The story means to rule out attempts to mitigate the severity of the law. No excuses! And of course, the point is not specifically to forbid the gathering of kindling on the Sabbath but to forbid any labor, great or small, hence the choice of a gnat instead of a camel (Matt. 23:24).

> And while the children of Israel were in the wilderness, they found a man gathering sticks upon the sabbath day. And they that found him gathering sticks brought him unto Moses and Aaron, and unto all the congregation. And they put him in ward, because it had not been declared what should be done to him. And Yahweh said unto Moses, The man shall surely be put to death: all the congregation shall stone him with stones without the camp. And all the congregation brought him without the camp, and stoned him to death with stones; as Yahweh commanded Moses. [Num. 15:32-36, ASV]

This story reminds one of the Shari'ah enforcement squads of Saudi Arabia, "neighborhood watch" committees always on the lookout for a woman showing a forbidden inch of ankle from beneath her burkha, and ready to pelt her with stones. The parallel tells us that such fanatical vigilance need not be dismissed as impossible, but we have reason to wonder if this statute was ever enforced.

We read that "the whole congregation" is to serve as executioner. This could never be done in the real world. Perhaps the elders of a village might act, or appoint some stone-slingers, but that is not what the text says. We begin to wonder if we are reading a code of laws that was ever promulgated.

It starts to sound like some fanatic's version of Plato's *Laws* or *The Republic:* a system of regulations existing only on paper, the way somebody thought things should be in an ideal theocracy. Think of the galaxy of stipulations produced by endless hours of rabbinical speculation to govern Jewish life. The attempt to live these laws out demands a closed subculture, a "finite province of meaning," [4] where everybody agrees to play by the rules and avoids contact with the surrounding culture that doesn't.

It is not unlike nerds busy in the basement with a role-playing game like

Dungeons and Dragons. We might wonder whether we are dealing with a set of rules intended to govern the behavior of only a pietistic sect like today's Hasidim. The laws mandating capital punishment are blanks in the firing chamber. Since these laws were propounded by Jews who lived under foreign domination, those who framed them must have known good and well that they could not have enforced the most severe of them (John 18:31, "It is not legal for us to put anyone to death.").

Their intent was to throw a scare into fellow Jews: "You're just lucky we're no longer in a position to enforce these!" The rabble was thus to appreciate the seriousness with which the pietists themselves took the rest of the laws. In short, the devout were drawing up rules and regulations to define piety and holiness so as to command the admiration of the rest of the people: "Wow! That's dedication! I'm glad *somebody's* being serious about the Torah!"

Accordingly, Josephus [5] tells us that the Pharisees were the most popular of the first-century Jewish sects. I suggest they were admired by the rest of the people, so to speak, for being pious *for them*, vicariously, and thus turning away the wrath of God against the common scofflaws.[6] The result would have been somewhat similar to Buddhism, where one admires the monks for a degree of holiness one cannot imagine attaining oneself. If one renders them financial support, it must at least count as a good work: "The one welcoming a prophet because he is a prophet will receive a prophet's wage, and the one welcoming a *zaddik* because he is a *zaddik* will receive a *zaddik's* wage" (Matt. 10:41).[7]

Numbers 12:1-16
Don't Question the Boss

Apologists for the accuracy of the gospels frequently point to the unflattering depictions of Simon Peter in those texts, contending that, given Peter's obvious importance in the early Christian movement, the only way such material could have made it into the gospels was if Peter himself had supplied it. Everyone else would have passed over such embarrassments in silence out of their reverence for the great man. But, trusting in Christ rather than his own scorecard, Peter must have been freely willing to tell tales out of school, even about himself, if it might help others to avoid the same errors of pride and obtuseness.

The apologetical mindset, akin to that of a political spin doctor, does not even envision the possibility that there were rival factions vying for prominence, authority, and membership, and one of the techniques employed to this end, as in politics today, was slander, vilification, and gossip. If I can indicate your figurehead's clay feet, I can undercut the authority of those who appeal to him for their pedigree. Paulinists told invidious tales about Peter, and Petrinists told them about Paul.[8] Numbers 12:1-16 is exactly this sort of ancient propaganda.

> And Miriam and Aaron spake against Moses because of the Cushite woman whom he had married; for he had married a Cushite woman. And they said, Hath Yahweh indeed spoken only with Moses? hath he not spoken also with us? And Yahweh heard it. Now the man Moses was very meek, above all the men that were upon the face of the earth. And Yahweh spake suddenly unto Moses, and unto Aaron, and unto Miriam, Come out ye three unto the tent of meeting. And they three came out. And Yahweh came down in a pillar of cloud, and stood at the door of the Tent, and called Aaron and Miriam; and they both came forth. And he said, Hear now my words: if there be a prophet among you, I Yahweh will make myself known unto him in a vision, I will speak with him in a dream. My servant Moses is not so; he is faithful in all my house: with him will I speak mouth to mouth, even manifestly, and not in dark speeches; and the form of Yahweh shall he behold: wherefore then were ye not afraid to speak against my servant, against Moses?
>
> And the anger of Yahweh was kindled against them; and he departed. And the cloud removed from over the Tent; and, behold, Miriam was leprous, as white as snow: and Aaron looked upon Miriam, and, behold, she was leprous. And Aaron said unto Moses, Oh, my lord, lay not, I pray thee, sin upon us, for that we have done foolishly, and for that we have sinned. Let her not, I pray, be as one dead, of whom the flesh is half consumed when he cometh out of his mother's womb. And Moses cried unto Yahweh, saying, Heal her, O God, I beseech thee. And Yahweh said unto Moses, If her father had but spit in her face, should she not be ashamed seven days? let her be shut up without the camp seven days, and after that she shall be brought in again. And Miriam was shut up without the camp seven days: and the people journeyed not till Miriam was brought in again. And afterward the people journeyed from Hazeroth, and encamped in the wilderness of Paran. [ASV]

It seems that Miriam and Aaron had a problem with their brother marrying a Cushite woman. It would be fascinating if the text intended an Ethiopian woman, since Cush was a name for Ethiopia or Abyssinia. But there was also a Cush in Asia Minor, but, as per Noth,[9] probably Cushan, near Midian, is intended here. The outcome of the complaint follows only in verses 9-15, where God gives Miriam a nasty case of leprosy for daring to mouth off against the Chosen One. As Noth[10] notes (!), the fact that Aaron comes away unscathed means that originally the story about Mosaic marriage meddling had only Miriam sticking her nose in.

Aaron did conspire with Miriam, however, in the other story jammed in here, the general challenge to Mosaic authority (verses 2-8). This is the sin that the reader/hearer is being warned to avoid. Now, Moses himself is understood to be long gone, so how can anyone in the storyteller's day even have the option of making this mistake? Of course, it is the irreproachability of some successors of Moses that is in question here. And Aaron and Miriam must represent such possible nit-pickers.

This makes sense on a purely literary level since one might imagine that only individuals so close to Moses would be in the position thus to criticize him. On the other hand, other stories do not hesitate to have the faceless collectivity of Israel complain against Moses with a single voice, as if a single character. It seems more likely that we are to read Aaron as representing the faction of priests, Miriam standing for the Levitical choristers (cf. Exod. 15:20-21), and Moses representing the scribes in charge of copying and interpreting the Torah. No one in this cast of characters stands for the prophets, though Moses' authority is exalted, rather disparagingly, over theirs.

This detail points to the lateness of the story: prophets no longer dare to show their faces (Zech. 13:2-6). The scribes have the final authority of Moses, as they interpret his law. Or at least so they claimed, and this is the story they told to underscore the point.

Numbers 16:1ff
Levitical Labor Disputes

Just as Luke 1:5, 8 depicts John the Baptist's father as belonging to one of the rotating divisions of priests chosen by lot to offer sacrifices, so the singers and musicians of the temple were divided into guilds, e.g., those of Asaph, Ethan, and others. Their names appear in the superscriptions attached to some of the Psalms. One of these guilds was the Sons of Korah.

Here is a tale of their eponymous (and presumably legendary) ancestor.

> Now Korah, the son of Izhar, the son of Kohath, the son of Levi,
> with Dathan and Abiram, the sons of Eliab, and On, the son of
> Peleth, sons of Reuben, took men: and they rose up before Moses,
> with certain of the children of Israel, two hundred and fifty princes
> of the congregation, called to the assembly, men of renown; and
> they assembled themselves together against Moses and against
> Aaron, and said unto them, Ye take too much upon you, seeing all
> the congregation are holy, every one of them, and Yahweh is
> among them: wherefore then lift ye up yourselves above the
> assembly of Yahweh? And when Moses heard it, he fell upon his
> face: and he spake unto Korah and unto all his company, saying, In
> the morning Yahweh will show who are his, and who is holy, and
> will cause him to come near unto him: even him whom he shall
> choose will he cause to come near unto him. This do: take you
> censers, Korah, and all his company; and put fire in them, and put
> incense upon them before Yahweh to-morrow: and it shall be that
> the man whom Yahweh doth choose, he shall be holy: ye take too
> much upon you, ye sons of Levi. And Moses said unto Korah, Hear
> now, ye sons of Levi: seemeth it but a small thing unto you, that
> the God of Israel hath separated you from the congregation of
> Israel, to bring you near to himself, to do the service of the
> tabernacle of Yahweh, and to stand before the congregation to
> minister unto them; and that he hath brought thee near, and all
> thy brethren the sons of Levi with thee? and seek ye the
> priesthood also? Therefore thou and all thy company are gathered
> together against Yahweh: and Aaron, what is he that ye murmur
> against him?
>
> And Moses sent to call Dathan and Abiram, the sons of Eliab; and
> they said, We will not come up: is it a small thing that thou hast
> brought us up out of a land flowing with milk and honey, to kill us
> in the wilderness, but thou must needs make thyself also a prince
> over us? Moreover thou hast not brought us into a land flowing
> with milk and honey, nor given us inheritance of fields and
> vineyards: wilt thou put out the eyes of these men? we will
> not come up.
>
> And Moses was very wroth, and said unto Yahweh, Respect not
> thou their offering: I have not taken one ass from them, neither

have I hurt one of them. And Moses said unto Korah, Be thou and all thy company before Yahweh, thou, and they, and Aaron, to-morrow: and take ye every man his censer, and put incense upon them, and bring ye before Yahweh every man his censer, two hundred and fifty censers; thou also, and Aaron, each his censer. And they took every man his censer, and put fire in them, and laid incense thereon, and stood at the door of the tent of meeting with Moses and Aaron. And Korah assembled all the congregation against them unto the door of the tent of meeting: and the glory of Yahweh appeared unto all the congregation.

And Yahweh spake unto Moses and unto Aaron, saying, Separate yourselves from among this congregation, that I may consume them in a moment. And they fell upon their faces, and said, O God, the God of the spirits of all flesh, shall one man sin, and wilt thou be wroth with all the congregation? And Yahweh spake unto Moses, saying, Speak unto the congregation, saying, Get you up from about the tabernacle of Korah, Dathan, and Abiram.

And Moses rose up and went unto Dathan and Abiram; and the elders of Israel followed him. And he spake unto the congregation, saying, Depart, I pray you, from the tents of these wicked men, and touch nothing of theirs, lest ye be consumed in all their sins. So they gat them up from the tabernacle of Korah, Dathan, and Abiram, on every side: and Dathan and Abiram came out, and stood at the door of their tents, and their wives, and their sons, and their little ones. And Moses said, Hereby ye shall know that Yahweh hath sent me to do all these works; for I have not done them of mine own mind. If these men die the common death of all men, or if they be visited after the visitation of all men; then Yahweh hath not sent me. But if Yahweh make a new thing, and the ground open its mouth, and swallow them up, with all that appertain unto them, and they go down alive into Sheol; then ye shall understand that these men have despised Yahweh.

And it came to pass, as he made an end of speaking all these words, that the ground clave asunder that was under them; and the earth opened its mouth, and swallowed them up, and their households, and all the men that appertained unto Korah, and all their goods. So they, and all that appertained to them, went down alive into Sheol: and the earth closed upon them, and they perished from among the assembly. And all Israel that were round about them fled at the cry of them; for they said, Lest the earth swallow us up. And fire came forth from Yahweh, and devoured the two hundred and fifty men that offered the incense.

And Yahweh spake unto Moses, saying, Speak unto Eleazar the son of Aaron the priest, that he take up the censers out of the burning, and scatter thou the fire yonder; for they are holy, even the censers of these sinners against their own lives; and let them be made beaten plates for a covering of the altar: for they offered them before Yahweh; therefore they are holy; and they shall be a sign unto the children of Israel. And Eleazar the priest took the brazen censers, which they that were burnt had offered; and they beat them out for a covering of the altar, to be a memorial unto the children of Israel, to the end that no stranger, that is not of the seed of Aaron, come near to burn incense before Yahweh; that he be not as Korah, and as his company: as Yahweh spake unto him by Moses.

But on the morrow all the congregation of the children of Israel murmured against Moses and against Aaron, saying, Ye have killed the people of Yahweh. And it came to pass, when the congregation was assembled against Moses and against Aaron, that they looked toward the tent of meeting: and, behold, the cloud covered it, and the glory of Yahweh appeared. And Moses and Aaron came to the front of the tent of meeting. And Yahweh spake unto Moses, saying, Get you up from among this congregation, that I may consume them in a moment. And they fell upon their faces. And Moses said unto Aaron, Take they censer, and put fire therein from off the altar, and lay incense thereon, and carry it quickly unto the congregation, and make atonement for them: for there is wrath gone out from Yahweh; the plague is begun. And Aaron took as Moses spake, and ran into the midst of the assembly; and, behold, the plague was begun among the people: and he put on the incense, and made atonement for the people. And he stood between the dead and the living; and the plague was stayed. [Num. 16:1-48, ASV]

Numbers 16:1a, 2-11, 16-21, 35-40 is a narrative monument to a sacerdotal labor dispute. The Korah guild are no longer satisfied with the duties to which the Levites had been reduced after the cult of Nehushtan was shut down.

The trouble was that, as mere singers and timbrel players, they could not offer animal sacrifices before Yahweh. The Aaronide priests did, and this meant they received the Grade-A leftover meat (that which was not burned up to feed Yahweh). These priestlings sought a promotion that would have entitled them to a share of sacrificial meat.

Picture them like the Israelite foremen gaining audience with Pharaoh to protest their working conditions in Exodus 5:15-51– only to get pretty much the same rude rebuff. Actually, worse, since Yahweh barbecues the poor bastards where they stand. *They* become burnt-offerings! The story makes it painfully clear that only the Aaronide priesthood has the right, and will ever have the right, to offer sacrifice–and to eat the steaks! (The death of Korah himself is not mentioned here because the redactor switched him to verse 32, so he could go down the chute with Dathan and Abiram. See below.)

Do we find their "sour grapes" rejoinder in Psalm 51:15-17? The Korahites lost their gambit. They had to swallow it, but they did manage to get their licks in, just as the resentful Nehushtan priest did when he cast the Serpent, his god, as the hero and the oppressive Yahweh as the villain in the Garden of Eden story. Somehow he got it past the censors, as did the author of this psalm:

O Lord [Adonai], open thou my lips,
  and my mouth shall show forth thy praise.
For thou hast no delight in sacrifice;
  were I to give a burnt offering, thou wouldst not be pleased.
The sacrifice acceptable to God is
  a broken spirit;
  a broken and contrite heart, O God, thou wilt not despise.

Ah, what do you know? Given the option of what Protestant Modernists called "the butcher shop religion" of the sacrificing priests on the one hand and the sincere contrition of the introspective heart, which do you think God must prefer? Of course, the latter, and that is just what the (hungry) Levitical choristers offer him. My house shall be called a house of prayer, but you have made it a slaughterhouse.

Verses 18-19 seem to constitute a later reinterpretation of verses 15-17.

Do good to Zion in thy good pleasure;
  rebuild the walls of Jerusalem,
  then wilt thou delight in right sacrifices,

> in burnt offerings and whole burnt offerings;
> then bulls will be offered on thy altar.

The nature of the contrast between the animal sacrifices and the sacrifice of repentance has changed. Now it is no longer that the latter is inherently superior to the former, which, if truth be told, God does not even want (cf. Jer. 7:22-23; Mic. 6:6-8). No, it is just that the temple and the altar of sacrifice have been swept away, and until these can be restored, God is happy to accept a broken spirit as a fit substitute for the real thing. This is not the same thing at all. Verses 18-19 seek to mute the heresy proclaimed in verses 15-17.

Another story, superficially similar, concerns Dathan and Abiram. It has been rather clumsily intercalated with the Korah story. But Dathan and Abiram are not jockeying for position. Instead, they are front men for the later, Judean, anti-Israel theme of murmuring and apostasy.

This one takes up verses 12-15, 23-34. Whereas the Korah story takes place at the Tent of Meeting (the Tabernacle), that of Dathan and Abiram is set at their tents. And the doom that befalls them is quite different and comes from below, not above: the earth's crust splits open to swallow them, giving them a one-way trip to the netherworld (as if Enoch or Elijah had stepped into the elevator and mistakenly hit the "down" button!).

Verses 41-49a, 50 represent a third story, another murmuring episode. Our redactor has taken the outcry of the malcontents ("You have killed the people of Yahweh!") as a protest at the deaths of fellow ingrates Dathan, Abiram, and their families, but I think it was merely another version of the ever- reiterated whining: "You've dragged us out here just to die in the desert!"

Yahweh decides another plague ought to knock some sense into them, and so he uses his bio-weapons like an ancient Saddam Hussein. Moses and Aaron, seeing what is developing, object that Yahweh cannot hold the whole people responsible for the transgression of a few (verse 22 originally belonged right here). With no apparent reply coming from the sulking deity, Moses and Aaron think fast: maybe a liberal sprinkling of incense (a kind of sacrifice) will atone for the sins of the people (who did after all sympathize with the big-mouth Dathan and Abiram) and stem the progress of the plague. And it works.

The scribe has tried to connect the three stories by adding names from each to the other: Dathan and Abiram in verse 1b, Korah in verses 24, 27, 32, and 49.

Numbers 17:1-11

Priesthood Reserved to Aaronides Alone

This one makes pretty much the same point as the Korah tale: The Aaronide priesthood has exclusive prerogatives, though no specific rival faction is named. But there is another dimension, as we will see.

> And Yahweh spake unto Moses, saying, Speak unto the children of Israel, and take of them rods, one for each fathers' house, of all their princes according to their fathers' houses, twelve rods: write thou every man's name upon his rod. And thou shalt write Aaron's name upon the rod of Levi; for there shall be one rod for each head of their fathers' houses. And thou shalt lay them up in the tent of meeting before the testimony, where I meet with you. And it shall come to pass, that the rod of the man whom I shall choose shall bud: and I will make to cease from me the murmurings of the children of Israel, which they murmur against you. And Moses spake unto the children of Israel; and all their princes gave him rods, for each prince one, according to their fathers' houses, even twelve rods: and the rod of Aaron was among their rods. And Moses laid up the rods before Yahweh in the tent of the testimony.
>
> And it came to pass on the morrow, that Moses went into the tent of the testimony; and, behold, the rod of Aaron for the house of Levi was budded, and put forth buds, and produced blossoms, and bare ripe almonds. And Moses brought out all the rods from before Yahweh unto all the children of Israel: and they looked, and took every man his rod. And Yahweh said unto Moses, Put back the rod of Aaron before the testimony, to be kept for a token against the children of rebellion; that thou mayest make an end of their murmurings against me, that they die not. Thus did Moses: as Yahweh commanded him, so did he. [Num. 17:1-11, ASV]

The episode doubles as a ceremonial etiology. It seeks to cover up a previous meaning of the budding rod in the Ark of the Covenant.

Traditional scholars and apologists were quite happy to embrace the old "Canaanite" dodge to distance supposedly pure-monotheistic Hebrew religion from the polytheism and idolatry on display throughout the Old Testament, as if all that had rubbed off from the Canaanites who survived the (fictive) genocidal blitzkrieg of Joshua. But no one would have wanted to write off the Ark of the Covenant as more degenerate syncretistic pollution. To be sure, it came in quite handy for apologetists to be able to show that other Near Eastern portable shrines are attested, so the Ark need not have been sheer fiction. Except Moses' Ark was constructed from a blueprint revealed to Moses atop Sinai. No room for Canaanite filching there!

But it does seem to stem from the polytheistic matrix of Old Testament religion. As Geo Widengren[11] has shown, the symbolism of the Ark and its contents correspond to the accoutrement of the Mesopotamian priest-kings. The tablets of the law may represent the Tablets of Destiny which the Near Eastern kings consulted each year, at the kingship renewal ceremony (in which the king became the earthly vicar of the divine king on earth), inside the Inner Sanctum of the temple. The budding rod was his scepter, symbolizing a twig or branch from the fabled Tree of Life in the garden of the gods. It served, too, as the wand wielded in the yearly ceremonial reenactment of the resurrection of the god.

Thus, both Moses and Aaron take the position of the ancient god-king. This does not mean that Moses was originally believed to be a king. But it does mean the whole business was borrowed from the cultures that had one. The model of borrowing from the adjacent peoples' religion turns out to be valid after all, once we realize that there were no ancient Israelite settlers to absorb all this from the Canaanites. Rather, the stories and symbols were borrowed, as literary tropes, from the resident cultures who had inherited them from their pasts in which god-kings did once actually rule. But, imported into Judaism, they had to be reinterpreted. This story gives us that reinterpretation.

2 Samuel 6:6-8

Touching the Ark

Excuse me for taking a side-trip over into 2 Samuel, but it provides an ideal example of the cautionary tale as directed to Levites. Numbers 4:15 warns those who transport the Ark and the attendant relics not to touch the "holy things" under pain of death. In this story, King David is having the Ark moved into Jerusalem in order to increase the holy clout of his new capital.[12] But there is an incident.

> And when they came to the threshing-floor of Nacon, Uzzah put forth his hand to the ark of God, and took hold of it; for the oxen stumbled. And the anger of Yahweh was kindled against Uzzah; and God smote him there for his error; and there he died by the

> ark of God. And David was displeased, because Yahweh had broken forth upon Uzzah; and he called that place Perez-uzzah, unto this day. [2 Sam. 6:6-8, ASV]

The ox cart carrying the Ark hits a pothole in the road and is teetering on the brink of a ditch. The zealous Levite Uzzah is panic-stricken that this holiest of all objects may suffer awful and ignominious defilement in the mud. So he reaches out to steady the imperiled Ark—and dies on the spot. Why? Because he touched the Ark!

This story purposely juxtaposes Uzzah's noble intentions with the severity of his trespass in order to clarify the issues. If the Almighty wants to uphold his Ark and keep it from getting muddy, he is fully able to do it, whether he deigns to or not. He doesn't need you to help him out of a jam! That would be even worse, because it would imply he is a helpless totem dependent on poor mortals like you and me. A modern parallel is found in an episode of *The Sopranos* where young Finn tries to pay for the family's meal at Vesuvio's, thinking he was getting in good with Meadow's dad. Tony's angry reaction—chewing him out and flinging hundred dollar bills on the table—is not what he expected.[13]

It is, I think, exactly the same point as that expressed in Isaiah 46:5-7. And it is a way of showing that God is not to be identified with his earthly throne, which would make it, and him, an idol.

But all this turns out to be a secondary layer added to what began as an etymological story. It seems that the name "Perez-uzzah" is a corruption of a name meaning "Mighty Zarephath," [14] but this has been lost sight of, and popular imagination doped out the phrase as meaning "breaking forth upon Uzzah." That was a gap that curiosity just had to fill. What, pray tell, broke forth upon someone named Uzzah? Must have been the wrath of God (cf. Exod. 19:22).

We can see the same process at work in Genesis 16:13-14: Hagar "said: 'Have I really seen God and remained alive after seeing him?' Therefore the well was called 'Beer-lahai-roi.'" The name actually means "well of the antelope's jawbone," a name denoting that the well could be found beside the landmark of a rising ridge of boulders suggesting a sun-bleached antelope jawbone. Evidently, someone did not know this and felt there must be a more theological definition and doped out the phrase as "the well of one who sees and lives." The story of Hagar followed as an explanation.

Gunkel supplies a perfect example of such popular etymology closer to home. "How many there are who believe that the noble river which runs down between New Hampshire and Vermont and across Massachusetts and Connecticut is so named because it 'connects' the first two and 'cuts' the latter two states!" [15]

Notes

1. The dugong is a cousin of the manatee. Good luck finding one in the middle of the Sinai Desert!

2. Think of the ecclesiastical fashion show in Fellini's *Roma*.

3. This one does not involve name origins, much less geological phenomena, but, as it is a prime scare story, this seems to be the best place to discuss it.

4. Peter L. Berger and Thomas Luckmann, *The Social Construction of Reality: A Treatise in the Sociology of Knowledge* (Garden City: Doubleday Anchor Books, 1967), p. 25.

5. Josephus, *Antiquities of the Jews*. In *The Works of Flavius* Josephus. Trans William Whiston (London: Ward, Lock, & Co., n.d.), p. 353.,XIII.X.6.

6. See Solomon Schechter, *Some Aspects of Rabbinic Theology* (NY: Macmillan, 1910), pp. 189-190, on the idea of "The *Zachuth* [merits] of a Pious Contemporary."

7. This one is my own translation, from my *The Pre-Nicene New Testament* (Salt Lake City: Signature Books, 2006).

8. Alfred Loisy, *The Birth of the Christian Religion*. Trans. L.P. Jacks (London: George Allen & Unwin, 1948), pp. 101-102.

9. Martin Noth, *Numbers: A Commentary*. Trans. James D. Martin. Old Testament Library (Philadelphia: Westminster Press, 1968) p. 94.

10. Noth, *Numbers*, p, 92. Sorry for yet another footNoth.

11. Geo Widengren, *The King and the Tree of Life in Ancient Near Eastern Religion*. King and Savior IV (Uppsala: A. B. Lundequistska Bokhandeln, 1951), p.39.

12. In Late Antiquity, urban bishops coveted the *mana* (the mojo?) of the increasingly numerous graves of saints and martyrs sprinkled about the countryside and eventually set about having the saints' relics exhumed and transferred to their churches, appropriating their numinous capital. See Peter Brown, *The Cult of the Saints: Its Rise and Function in Latin Christianity* . Haskell Lectures on History of Religions; new series, no. 2 (Chicago: University of Chicago Press, 1981), pp. 32-33, 36-37, 42, 123. David is pictured as pursuing the same strategy: the Ark would henceforth stay put in its new home. And obviously that was the strategy of King Josiah in the story of his shutting down all the local hilltop shrines and sacred groves in favor of the Jerusalem temple. As L. Sprague de Camp suggested in his novel *The Dragon of the Ishtar Gate* (NY: Lancer Books, 1968), such centralization was likely motivated as much by monopolism as by monotheism, an attempt to corner the market of offerings

for the Yahweh priests of Jerusalem.

13. "Unidentified Black Males," *The Sopranos*, Season 5, Episode 9.

14. T.K. Cheyne, "Perez-uzzah," *Encyclopedia Biblica*, cols. 3654-3655.

15. Gunkel, *Legends of Genesis*, p. 28.

Chapter Four

Murmuring Mouths and Babbling Brooks

The stories in this chapter exhibit two very different themes. As George W. Coats demonstrated in a fascinating form- and tradition-critical monograph,[1] these tales of local oases, their origins and names, were first taken up into a larger tradition meant to illustrate Yahweh's protection and provision for his elect people during their time in the wilderness. The people make known their needs, and their God meets them.

There is little rancor, only initial distress. And, following Noth,[2] I should think that in this early stage of the tradition, Moses had not yet been added as Israel's mediator with Yahweh. The people cried out, and God heard them.

As pictured here, as Jeremiah (2:2-3; cf. Hos. 2:14-20; 9:10) had said, the sojourn in the wilderness was a honeymoon period when God rejoiced to attend to his new bride's needs. But subsequently, already before J's compilation, someone had retold the stories, adding the motif of a bitter, recurring, and wholesale repudiation by Israel of Yahweh and Moses. Now the people (speaking in the artificial manner of a folktale, in unison as if a single character)[3] bemoan that Moses ever dragged them out of Egypt where, comparatively speaking, things were pretty good! It is this ungrateful recalcitrance that leads an exasperated Yahweh to condemn the Israelites to drop dead in the desert, never to set sandal in the Promised Land.

Coats argues that this redacted wilderness narrative embodies the same agenda as Psalm 78, a gloating rehash, not so much of "the mighty acts of God" as of the miserable acts of the apostates, the Northern Kingdom of Israel. Remember how the story of the guilty Aaron and the Golden Calf coincided with the words of Israelite King Jeroboam at his unveiling of the calf/bull statues of Yahweh ("who brought you out of Egypt")? The way the redactor rewrote and reused that story implied that Jeroboam's breakaway kingdom in the north, which remained independent of Davidic Judah to the south, had already lapsed into irrevocable idolatry and apostasy. Thus it had long since lost divine favor, as early as Jeroboam, as early as Aaron.

The redactional overlay of the murmuring motif argues that only Judah in the south retains God's blessing and election as the people of God. This is the point of the story of the spies' reconnaissance mission in Canaan, where most of them, faithless cowards, urge Moses to find someplace else to conquer: these Canaanites are too formidable! Caleb (eponymous ancestor of one of the main clans in Judah) is the only one to protest that, trusting in God, they can take the Canaanites (Num. 13:30). This is a wink to the hearer or reader that Caleb's descendants, i.e., the Kingdom of Judah, will one day rule with the divine mandate (Num. 14:20-24) while Israel to the north will wind up as one more notch on the Assyrian gun belt. (Joshua[4] has been added to this story as an afterthought, in the interests of making this story anticipate the Conquest.)

The J version of the murmuring episodes, then, are aimed at vilifying Judah's rival kingdom in favor of the Davidic dynasty. They imply God has abrogated the covenant he made with Moses and Israel in favor of a new covenant with the dynasty of David in Judah (2 Sam. 7:12-15; Pss. 89:19-38). But Archaeology makes it clear that there is as little evidence for the Davidic-Solomonic Empire or their magnificent (albeit airy) structures as there is for the exodus or for the Nephite civilization.

Does that development undermine Coats's analysis, presented here? I think not. Remember how long the north-south rivalry lasted. At least into the New Testament period, when Jews and Samaritans would not stoop to eat off each other's crockery (John 4:9). Judean Pharisees (the only kind there were) disdained the Torah-ignorance and apathy of Galilean hillbillies. These stories would still have plenty of use left in them. And they need not have begun in the royal courts of Judah (which we now know didn't exist).

Remember, according to the legends, David's monarchy began by appropriating the priest-king office of Jerusalem, and his successors were said to inherit this dignity: "Yahweh has sworn, nor will he change his mind: you are a priest in perpetuity, of the Order of Melchizedek" (Pss. 110:4). There may never have been actual kings of Judah, but the high priests styled themselves as kings, wearing royal vestments and dispensing what justice their Gentile overlords left to them. They were a "royal priesthood" (1 Pet. 2:9). The Zadokite priests [5] cherished their pedigree as David's preferred clergy. So it is not hard to see that the Jewish priesthood would have created a tradition of rival kingdoms: one faithful and the other apostate, one Davidic and the other Mosaic.

Traditionally we have harmonized all these covenants in some sort of dispensational schema, but that is not the original intent. The compilers of the Bible are responsible for the harmonization; it has taken us this long to recognize it and to separate the original elements, a procedure closely akin to distinguishing the Yahwist, Elohist, Deuteronomic, and Priestly sources. Think of how physicists first isolated protons, neutrons, and electrons, thinking they had finished the job–until they realized these entities could be broken down further into mesons, neutrinos, and that whole subatomic zoo.

I have already said that the wilderness traditions did not anticipate an abandonment of nomadism for a settled, agricultural existence in Canaan. In the wilderness stories, the children of Israel were going in circles because they *wanted* to. They were nomadic shepherds who annually made the rounds of oases and grazing areas. That's just the kind of life they led.

Though he is a secondary addition to those stories, Moses belongs in them. He was the shepherd of Israel in Israel's proper home: the desert. Joshua is the hero of the Conquest saga. Abraham and Jacob were the patriarchal heroes, and the promises (e.g., Gen. 12:7; 17:7-8) their god(s) made to them were simply (fictive) real estate guarantees: Their descendants would own these lands in perpetuity.

When we look at the later elaborations of those promises (e.g., Gen. 15:13-16) it becomes overwhelmingly obvious that harmonizing compilers have stuffed into the earlier accounts elaborate summaries-in-advance of the exodus in order to knit the Patriarchal cycle into the exodus cycle. These various covenants made with Abraham, Moses, and David have been only artificially placed in a sequence. Even at that, they do not fit together. Each is a "new covenant" supplanting the one placed before it. Of course, anticipations and harmonizations are peppered throughout the unified text, but these are as fully contrived as the New Testament retrospective reinterpretations of Old Testament passages as if they were pointing to Jesus.

Exodus 16:1-36

Manna from Heaven, Diet of Worms

We can sniff out three layers of narration in the famous story of the manna in the wilderness. The first is both an etymology and an etiology for "traveller's bread," a honey-dew excretion by desert insects on the ubiquitous tamarisk trees. The story depicts the delight of weary desert travelers upon discovering the tasty stuff. The wondering exclamation, "What is it?" (Hebrew *manna*) supplies the name.

The miracle both supplies the imagined origin and betrays the story teller's lack of first-hand acquaintance with the conditions of the desert, since he imagines the stuff was miraculously delivered every day from the sky. Subsequently, someone decided to appropriate (and elaborate) the story as a ceremonial story: Yahweh provides the manna as an object lesson on Sabbath observance.

Finally, a Judean scribe has introduced the murmuring motif to incriminate the northerners who had already begun to repudiate the covenant Yahweh had made with them as of the exodus. How they pine for the good old days in Egypt! What a mistake, or even a malicious trick, it was for Yahweh to drag them out to the wilderness, without so much as a mirage in sight! One must compare the stiff-necked heard-heartedness of the Israelites in the murmuring propaganda tales to the preternatural stubbornness of Pharaoh: What will it take to get the message through?

And they took their journey from Elim, and all the congregation of the children of Israel came unto the wilderness of Sin, which is between Elim and Sinai, on the fifteenth day of the second month after their departing out of the land of Egypt. And the whole congregation of the children of Israel murmured against Moses and against Aaron in the wilderness: and the children of Israel said unto them, Would that we had died by the hand of Yahweh in the land of Egypt, when we sat by the flesh-pots, when we did eat bread to the full; for ye have brought us forth into this wilderness, to kill this whole assembly with hunger.

Then said Yahweh unto Moses, Behold, I will rain bread from heaven for you; and the people shall go out and gather a day's portion every day, that I may prove them, whether they will walk in my law, or not. And it shall come to pass on the sixth day, that they shall prepare that which they bring in, and it shall be twice as much as they gather daily. And Moses and Aaron said unto all the children of Israel, At even, then ye shall know that Yahweh hath brought you out from the land of Egypt; and in the morning, then ye shall see the glory of Yahweh; for that he heareth your murmurings against Yahweh: and what are we, that ye murmur against us? And Moses said, This shall be, when Yahweh shall give you in the evening flesh to eat, and in the morning bread to the full; for that Yahweh heareth your murmurings which ye murmur against him: and what are we? your murmurings are not against us, but against Yahweh.

And Moses said unto Aaron, Say unto all the congregation of the children of Israel, Come near before Yahweh; for he hath heard your murmurings. And it came to pass, as Aaron spake unto the whole congregation of the children of Israel, that they looked toward the wilderness, and, behold, the glory of Yahweh appeared in the cloud. And Yahweh spake unto Moses, saying, I have heard the murmurings of the children of Israel: speak unto them, saying, At even ye shall eat flesh, and in the morning ye shall be filled with bread: and ye shall know that I am Yahweh your God.

And it came to pass at even, that the quails came up, and covered the camp: and in the morning the dew lay round about the camp. And when the dew that lay was gone up, behold, upon the face of the wilderness a small round thing, small as the hoar-frost on the ground. And when the children of Israel saw it, they said one to another, What is it? For they knew not what it was. And Moses said unto them, It is the bread which Yahweh hath given you to eat. This is the thing which Yahweh hath commanded, Gather ye of it every man according to his eating; an omer a head, according to the number of your persons, shall ye take it, every man for them that are in his tent. And the children of Israel did so, and gathered some more, some less. And when they measured it with an omer, he that gathered much had nothing over, and he that gathered little had no lack; they gathered every man according to his eating. And Moses said unto them, Let no man leave of it till the morning. Notwithstanding they hearkened not unto Moses; but some of them left of it until the morning, and it bred worms, and became foul: and Moses was wroth with them. And they gathered it morning by morning, every man according to his eating: and when the sun waxed hot, it melted.

And it came to pass, that on the sixth day they gathered twice as much bread, two omers for each one: and all the rulers of the congregation came and told Moses. And he said unto them, This is that which Yahweh hath spoken, Tomorrow is a solemn rest, a holy sabbath unto Yahweh: bake that which ye will bake, and boil that which ye will boil; and all that remaineth over lay up for you to be kept until the morning. And they laid it up till the morning, as Moses bade: and it did not become foul, neither was there any worm therein. And Moses said, Eat that to-day; for to-day is a sabbath unto Yahweh: to-day ye shall not find it in the field. Six days ye shall gather it; but on the seventh day is the sabbath, in it there shall be none. And it came to pass on the seventh day, that there went out some of the people to gather, and they found none.

And Yahweh said unto Moses, How long refuse ye to keep my commandments and my laws? See, for that Yahweh hath given you the sabbath, therefore he giveth you on the sixth day the bread of two days; abide ye every man in his place, let no man go out of his place on the seventh day. So the people rested on the seventh day.

And the house of Israel called the name thereof Manna: and it was like coriander seed, white; and the taste of it was like wafers made with honey. And Moses said, This is the thing which Yahweh hath commanded, Let an omerful of it be kept throughout your generations, that they may see the bread wherewith I fed you in the wilderness, when I brought you forth from the land of Egypt. And Moses said unto Aaron, Take a pot, and put an omerful of manna therein, and lay it up before Yahweh, to be kept throughout your generations. As Yahweh commanded Moses, so Aaron laid it up before the Testimony, to be kept. And the children of Israel did eat the manna forty years, until they came to a land inhabited; they did eat the manna, until they came unto the borders of the land of Canaan. Now an omer is the tenth part of an ephah. [Exod. 16:1-36, ASV]

The quails in verses 8, 12-13 seem to be a clumsy addition to the story, which clearly means for the provision of the manna to be the solution to the people's hunger. After all, God's announcement that he will provide bread next morning says nothing about meat. If you're planning on serving steak, are you only going to mention the rolls? Why blur the focus? Because some pedantic scribe noticed the mention of nostalgia, not only for Egyptian bread (16:3), but also for the fleshpots of Egypt and decided that if Yahweh was to show he could go Egypt one better, he would have to provide meat as well.

Numbers 11:1-3
The Name "Taberah"

Barely enough of a story is told here as to supply an explanation for the place name *Taberah*, "burning."

And the people were as murmurers, speaking evil in the ears of Yahweh: and when Yahweh heard it, his anger was kindled; and the fire of Yahweh burnt among them, and devoured in the uttermost part of the camp. And the people cried unto Moses; and

Moses prayed unto Yahweh, and the fire abated. And the name of that place was called Taberah, because the fire of Yahweh burnt among them. [Num. 11:1-3, ASV]

What is the story doing here, almost as a preface to the story of the quails? I suspect that the compiler had on hand an etymology for an alternate location of the quail story. According to this one, the place had been named Taberah because that's where Yahweh blew a fuse, as he so often does in these dismal tales. The original cause was the grousing about the menu, used in the quail story, and no new, specific occasion was supplied here.

One cannot help suspecting that the stock phrase "the wrath of Yahweh was *kindled*" (also occurring in Num. 11:33; cf. also "the anger of Yahweh blazed hotly" in 11:10) has been literalized here, making Yahweh a vindictive arsonist, and the name "Taberah" is supposed to commemorate this, as a warning to hearers not to get Yahweh riled up. The compiler just didn't want to leave "Taberah" on the cutting room floor. (One might almost say that what we have here is a case of Noth's redundancy principle applied, not to a character, but to a place!) Might Taberah ("burning") have originally been a place, like Tophet (Jer. 7:31-32; 19:13; 2 Kings 23:10), where infant sacrifices were offered by fire?

Numbers 11:10, 13, 18-23, 31-33
The Plague of Quails

First off, a redactor has spliced together a story about God's provision of quails with the account of the ordination of the seventy elders. This is evident from the fact that Moses' complaint to God that he cannot bear the burden of his people alone has nothing to do with the circumstance that supposedly prompted his complaint.

How is the appointment of a lower court of seventy men supposed to help Moses solve the food crisis? No, the original point of Moses' complaint must have been that deciding so many small claims cases every day was wearing him out. This version of the same story as found in Exodus chapter 18 simply transfers Jethro's concern (Exod. 18:13-18) about Moses to Moses' own mouth: he risks burn-out. So we need to bracket this portion of the text and discuss it separately.

The core of the story of the quails can be seen preserved in Numbers 11:10a, 11a, 13, 23, 31-32:

Moses heard the people weeping throughout their families, every man at the door of his own tent.

Moses said to Yahweh, "Where am I to get meat to give to all these people? [6] For they weep before me and say, 'Give us meat that we may eat!'"

And Yahweh said to Moses, "Is Yahweh's hand shortened? Now you shall see whether my word [of promised provision] will come true for you or not."

And there went forth a wind from Yahweh,[7] and it brought quails from the sea and let them fall beside the camp, and about two cubits above the face of the earth. And the people rose all that day, and all night, and all the next day, and gathered the quails; he who gathered least gathered ten homers; and they spread them out for themselves all around the camp. [Num. 11:10, 13, 23, 31-32, ASV]

We may wonder, with Noth, if even this version is already embellished by the addition of Moses, since it makes perfect sense if the story originally had Yahweh himself hear the weeping of his hungry people. At this stage, the story is, as Coats argues, purely a story of God living up to his promises to the people he had delivered. He once heard their groanings under the whips of the Egyptian slave-drivers (Exod. 3:7-8); even so, now he will attend to their looming starvation. And he does.

Once Moses has crept into the story, his only role is to supply a stock feature of miracle stories, the element of initial skepticism[8] which lifts the bar higher, making the miracle all the more triumphant when it happens. "After I have grown old, and my husband is old, shall I have pleasure?" (Gen. 18:12). "Teacher, do you not care if we perish?" (Mark 4:38) "You see the crowd pressing around you, and yet you say, 'Who touched me?'" (Mark 5:31). "And they laughed at him" (Mark 5:40). "How are we to buy bread, so that these people may eat?" (John 6:5).

As Coats suggests, another layer has been added to the story, making the Israelites a bunch of griping ingrates who rue the day Yahweh yanked them out of good old Egypt:

The people of Israel. . . wept again and said, "O that we had meat to eat! We remember the fish we ate in Egypt for nothing, the cucumbers, the melons, the leeks, the onions, and the garlic; but now our strength is dried up, and there is nothing at all but this manna to look at." [9] Now the manna was like coriander seed and its appearance like that of bdellium. The people went about and gathered it, and ground it in mills or beat it in mortars and boiled it in pots and made cakes of it. And the taste of it was like the taste of cakes baked with oil. When the dew fell upon the camp in the night, the manna fell with it. . . . [And Yahweh said to Moses,] "And say to the people, 'Consecrate yourselves for tomorrow, and you shall eat meat, for you have wept in the hearing of [Yahweh], saying, "Who will give us meat to eat? For it was well with us in Egypt." Therefore [Yahweh] will give you meat, and you shall eat. You shall not eat one day, or two days, or five days, or ten days, or twenty days, but a whole month until it comes out at your nostrils and becomes loathsome to you, because you have rejected [Yahweh] who is among you and have wept before him, saying, "Why did we come forth out of Egypt?"'" But Moses said, 'The people among whom I am number six hundred thousand on foot, and you have said, "I will give them meat that they may eat a whole month"? Shall flocks and herds be slaughtered for them, to suffice them? Or shall all the fish of the sea be gathered together for them, to suffice them?' (Num. 11:4-9, 18-22, English Standard Version).

We find the final layer in the opening and closing verses, where the story is repurposed to explain the place name "Graves of Craving." [10] "Now the rabble that was among them had a strong craving. . . and said, 'O that we had meat to eat!' . . . While the meat was yet between their teeth, before it was consumed, the anger of [Yahweh] was kindled against the people, and [Yahweh] smote the people with a very great plague. Therefore the name of that place was called Kibroth-hatta-avah, because there they buried the people who had the craving" (Num. 11:4, 33-34, ESV).

Notice how Numbers 11:4a blames but a segment of Israel for the fatal bellyaching: "Now the rabble that was among them had a strong craving," and verse 34 repeats the "craving": "Therefore the name of that place was called Kibroth-hatta-avah, because there they buried the people who had the craving" (ESV). Again, it was a few bad apples, not the whole barrel.

A redactional seam is visible back in verse 4 where this etymological frame has been affixed to the larger story: "and the people of Israel also wept again," etc. For this framing material, it was only a small number of malcontents who paid for it with their lives, whereas in the larger story, it is, as Coats observes, the whole congregation who reject Yahweh, wishing Yahweh had never effected the exodus in the first place. The conflation of these two stories explains the vicious portrayal of the peevish deity. It is only the etymological anecdote (originally the same size as the adjacent and similar tale of how Taberah got its name in Num. 11:1-3) that has Yahweh kill the complainers. The rest of the story has Yahweh tell them they are going to get just as sick and tired of the same quail as they had become of the manna. There's no pleasing some people!

The reference to the manna (11:7-9) is obviously an afterthought, imported from the Exodus 16 version. Why insert it here? Simply to up the quotient of the people's ingratitude: "That damn manna! Can't stand the sight of it anymore!" They had to learn the hard way that beggars can't be choosers. "So the bread of angels isn't good enough for you, eh?"

Exodus 15:22-25
Sweet Waters at Marah

It is natural that an acrid water source would come to be known as "Bitterness" (Hebrew: *marah*). But why would anyone give such a name to water that tasted sweet?

> And Moses led Israel onward from the Red Sea, and they went out into the wilderness of Shur; and they went three days in the wilderness, and found no water. And when they came to Marah, they could not drink of the waters of Marah, for they were bitter: therefore the name of it was called Marah. And the people murmured against Moses, saying, What shall we drink? An he cried unto Yahweh; And Yahweh showed him a tree, and he cast it into the waters, and the waters were made sweet. There he made for them a statute and an ordinance, and there he proved them [Exod. 15:22-25, ASV]

A drinkable spring named "Bitterness" seemed to demand a story in which someone performed the miracle of making bitter water sweet. (Elisha performs the same feat at Jericho in 2 Kings 2:19-22.) One wonders if the name originally denoted a place of ritual lamentation and mourning, recalling the sacred grave of Deborah, Rebecca's nurse, called Allon-bacuth, "Oak of Weeping." Also, think of Psalm 139:1, "By the waters of Babylon, there we sat down and wept, when we remembered Zion."

Verse 24 is another instance of shoe-horning the murmuring motif into a simple story of need and provision.

Exodus 17:1-7

Wellsprings at Massah and Meribah

These names mean, respectively, "proof" and "contention." Presumably they marked the oasis as a site for legal arbitration. People would make the journey there to set their disputes before a local oracle priest who, like Moses in Exodus 15:22, would enter a dissociative state and allow the babbling of the brooks to stir his subconscious. In other words, he would hear the sounds of the water as the words of God or Baal or whomever.

Why there? Pools, springs, and groves were believed to be the dwelling places of local deities, saints, and djinn. What else could explain the existence of such a well-watered and shady spot in the midst of the surrounding barrenness? They were local Edens, gardens of the gods. So if you wanted your claims settled, that's where you went.

> And all the congregation of the children of Israel journeyed from the wilderness of Sin, by their journeys, according to the commandment of Yahweh, and encamped in Rephidim: and there was no water for the people to drink. Wherefore the people stove with Moses, and said, Give us water that we may drink. And Moses said unto them, Why strive ye with me? Wherefore do ye tempt Yahweh? And the people thirsted there for water; and the people murmured against Moses, and said, Wherefore hast thou brought us up out of Egypt, to kill us and our children and our cattle with thirst? And Moses cried unto Yahweh, saying, What shall I do unto this people? They are almost ready to stone me.

> And Yahweh said unto Moses, Pass on before the people, and take with thee of the elders of Israel; and they rod, wherewith thou smotest the river, take in thy hand, and go. Behold, I will stand before thee there upon the rock in Horeb; and thou shalt smite the rock, and there shall come water out of it, that the people may drink. And Moses did so in the sight of the elders of Israel. And he called the name of the place Massah, and Meribah, because of the striving of the children of Israel, and because they tempted Yahweh, saying, Is Yahweh among us, or not? [Exod. 17:1-7, ASV]

Verses 1 and 5-6 give us the first layer of the text, a geological story to explain the origin of the oasis, replacing the older belief that local deities lived in the place. Now it is a miracle of Moses. But here comes the murmuring business again in verses 2-4, 7, and with it comes a new name origin that marks the place as a site of Israel's rebellion—as if anyone at the time would actually name a place for a spiritual failure.

The Old Testament provides other geological myths of the same type. God causes a spring to burst forth at Lehi to refresh Samson. After a long day of braining Philistines with a donkey's jawbone, it was Miller Time (Judges 15:18-19).

Numbers 20:1-13

Here is a complete retelling of the Massah and Meribah story (leaving out the redundant Massah) from the standpoint of the murmuring motif. This time the whole story vilifies Israel.

> And the children of Israel, even the whole congregation, came into the wilderness of Zin in the first month: and the people abode in Kadesh; and Miriam died there, and was buried there. And there was no water for the congregation: and they assembled themselves together against Moses and against Aaron. And the people strove with Moses, and spake, saying, Would that we had died when our brethren died before Yahweh! And why have ye brought the assembly of Yahweh into this wilderness, that we should die there, we and our beasts? And wherefore have ye made us to come up out of Egypt, to bring us in unto this evil place? it is no place of seed, or of figs, or of vines, or of pomegranates; neither is there any water to drink. And Moses and Aaron went from the presence of the assembly unto the door of the tent of meeting, and fell upon their faces: and the glory of Yahweh appeared unto them. And Yahweh spake unto Moses, saying, Take the rod, and assemble the congregation, thou, and Aaron thy brother, and speak ye unto the rock before their eyes, that it give forth its water; and thou shalt bring forth to them water out of the rock; so thou shalt give the congregation and their cattle drink. And Moses took the rod from before Yahweh, as he commanded him.

> And Moses and Aaron gathered the assembly together before the rock, and he said unto them, Hear now, ye rebels; shall we bring you forth water out of this rock? And Moses lifted up his hand, and smote the rock with his rod twice: and water came forth abundantly, and the congregation drank, and their cattle. And Yahweh said unto Moses and Aaron, Because ye believed not in me, to sanctify me in the eyes of the children of Israel, therefore ye

shall not bring this assembly into the land which I have given them. These are the waters of Meribah; because the children of Israel strove with Yahweh, and he was sanctified in them. [Num. 20:1-13, ASV]

What does this version of the story add? Of course, the new feature is Moses' hot-headed disobedience and punishment. It seems that Yahweh became greatly upset at Moses smacking the rock to get water out of it (even though Yahweh actually commanded him to hit the rock in the other version). What's the difference? And why does God fly off the handle at such a trivial infraction?

This is why: There were no stories of Moses or the wilderness generation entering the Promised Land because, again, the stories presuppose a nomadic existence. The notion of the Israelites merely passing through the wasteland to get to Canaan is a harmonization of the desert stories and the conquest legend. Moses has been sprinkled liberally into desert stories (and even plague stories) from which he had originally been absent, so why not just write him into the conquest stories? Because these stories were Joshua stories, and he was an epic hero in his own right. No one wanted to displace him with Moses. So Moses could not be depicted as crossing the Jordan and entering into Canaan.

But once the two cycles of stories have been artificially fused together, some reason must be found (created) for Moses never entering the Promised Land. Something extraordinary must have prevented what would naturally have occurred. What could it have been? Maybe he committed some sin. After all, that is what caused God to shut the griping Israelites out. But they were disgraceful apostates, and Moses cannot be tarred with that brush. So a minor infraction is trumped up for him. Even a slight misstep is enough to arouse Yahweh's vengeful ire, so it didn't seem implausible. Remember, God was the object of holy terror. As Harry Emerson Fosdick quipped, "One does not go into one's room and shut the door to commune in secret with such a deity." [11]

Numbers 21:1-3
The Name "Hormah"

"Hormah" means destruction, so it was inevitable that some story of destruction would be spun out to justify the name.

And the Canaanite, the king of Arad, who dwelt in the South, heard tell that Israel came by the way of Atharim; and he fought against Israel, and took some of them captive. And Israel vowed a vow unto Yahweh, and said, If thou wilt indeed deliver this people into my hand, then I will utterly destroy their cities. And Yahweh hearkened to the voice of Israel, and delivered up the Canaanites; and they utterly destroyed them and their cities: and the name of the place was called Hormah. [Num. 21:1-3, ASV]

What is most significant for our purposes is that Moses does not figure into this story at all. It shows how unnecessary he is in any of these stories, implying, a la Noth, that originally the tales depicted only Yahweh and Israel. Israel as a collective character makes a vow to Yahweh. Why did no one think to insert Moses here, as in the rest of the stories? Probably simple "editorial fatigue" again, especially given the brevity of the story. It was easy to miss, and to skip.

Notes

1. George W. Coats, *Rebellion in the Wilderness: The Murmuring Motif in the Wilderness Traditions of the Old Testament* (NY: Abingdon Press, 1968).

2. Noth, *History of Pentateuchal Traditions*, pp. 166-167.

3. Gunkel, *Legends of Genesis*, pp. 49-50.

4. Joshua is very likely an idealized version of the Judean King Josiah, who conquered some territory from Israel to the north.

5. Is it possible to suggest that the "Zadokite" priesthood was originally the same as the Melchi-*zedek* priesthood, both after all, associated with David?

6. Compare the retort of the disciples in Mark 6:37 and 8:4, which are retellings of this Moses story.

7. Remember, he is, like Zeus, Thor, Indra, Marduk, and Baal, a storm god.

8. Gerd Theissen, *The Miracle Stories of the Early Christian Tradition* Trans. Francis McDonagh (Philadelphia: Fortress Press, 1983), "Skepticism and Mockery," p. 56.

9. "Bread of heaven, bread of heaven, feed me till I want no more!"

10. Cf., Prov. 30:15-16, "Three things are never satisfied. Four never say, 'Enough!' Sheol, the barren womb, the earth ever thirsty for water, and the fire which never says, 'Enough!'"

11. Harry Emerson Fosdick, *A Guide to Understanding the Bible* (NY: Harper & Row, 1933; Torchbook ed., 1956), p. 210.

Chapter Five
Ethnological Stories

Exodus 17:8-16
Animosity towards Amalekites

Here is classic Old Testament grudge theology. It not only seeks to account for the sorry history between Israel and the Amalekites; it also signals a self-fulfilling resignation to the notion that the future must and will be a replay of the past.

> Then came Amalek, and fought with Israel in Rephidim. And Moses said unto Joshua, Choose us out men, and go out, fight with Amalek: to-morrow I will stand on the top of the hill with the rod of God in my hand. So Joshua did as Moses had said to him, and fought with Amalek: and Moses, Aaron, and Hur went up to the top of the hill. And it came to pass, when Moses held up his hand, that Israel prevailed; and when he let down his hand, Amalek prevailed. But Moses' hands were heavy; and they took a stone, and put it under him, and he sat thereon; and Aaron and Hur stayed up his hands, the one on the one side, and the other on the other side; And his hands were steady until the going down of the sun. And Joshua discomfited Amalek and his people with the edge of the sword.
>
> And Yahweh said unto Moses, Write this for a memorial in a book, and rehearse it in the ears of Joshua: that I will utterly blot out the remembrance of Amalek from under heaven. And Moses built an altar, and called the name of it Jehovah-nissi; And he said, Yahweh hath sworn: Yahweh will have war with Amalek from generation to generation. [Exod. 17:8-16, ASV]

Noth spots no less than four anomalies here. First, the rod (magic wand) of Moses is mentioned at the start but quickly forgotten: It is not the rod (in one hand) that does the trick but rather his upraised hands.[1] Second, Aaron and Hur would be good candidates for Noth's redundancy principle: Their role here is strictly secondary, so that we must suspect they have been elbowed aside from the central role they once played in an earlier version of the tale.[2] Third, why did the battle take all day if Moses' miraculous power was at work?[3] Fourth, there seems to be some confusion between the rock on which Moses parked his posterior and the altar he had built to commemorate the victory.[4]

Here is a possible way of sorting things out, submitted for your approval: Suppose the Moses story originally depicted Moses lifting his wand aloft, but inevitably becoming fatigued. The spirit is willing, but the flesh is weak. The tide of battle would turn until he felt he could lift the rod again. This happened over and over again, which explains how, despite Moses' powers (Yahweh is never mentioned!), the battle lasted so long.

But someone thought to mitigate the depiction of Moses' weakness and so added Aaron, who had Moses sit on the stone and kept his arm in place when Moses' stamina failed. Moses' rod was still the instrument of power in this version. This story was invoked to (re-)explain the sacred flat rock on the hilltop, which had previously possessed some pagan significance, perhaps, analogous to the Ark of the Covenant, serving as the throne of some local Baal who sat there, invisible to all but the hierophant who heard and conveyed his oracles to paying inquirers.

Then someone spiced the story together with an independent story in which the mysterious Hur was the hero, with Moses nowhere in sight. My guess is that the battle was going badly, with no supernatural intervention, until Hur lifted high a battle standard and cried out "A hand on the banner of Yahweh!" Perhaps he had grabbed up a banner fallen from the hands of a slain compatriot. The Israelite host, thus inspired, rallied and won the victory. And to commemorate it, the victors built an altar, naming it with Hur's heroic battle cry. Our compiler did not care to lionize some subordinate hero and so incorporated the story of Hur into the Moses tale. Now the only role left to Hur was to hold up Moses' other hand, and this occasioned the disappearance of the rod from the story; now it is simply Moses' upraised hands that do the trick.

Numbers 25:1-18

Mixing with (and up) Moabites and Midianites

This section combines three different traditions and/or earlier texts. One has Yahweh command Moses to tell the "judges" (presumably his "lower court" subordinates) to see to the slaughter of Israelites who partook in Moabite worship (orgies?). Another brief note tells how Yahweh commanded Moses to crucify those same judges as a vicarious atonement for the sins of the people: Yahweh will accept their deaths as sufficient. What were the sins? Who had committed them? In the present context we are to suppose Yahweh was enraged at the people's dalliance with Moabite Baal worship, but, originally, who knows?

Yet another piece of the puzzle has Aaron's grandson (and eventual successor) Phineas atone for the people's sins by skewering a mixed couple, an Israelite man named Zimri and his Midianite wife Cozbi. Just as the Levites had distinguished themselves and earned priestly prerogatives by violence against Israelite apostates (Exod. 32:25-29), so now the line of Phineas owed their position to the fanatical zeal of their eponymous forbear.

And what was the capital offense of the unhappy couple? It is hard to imagine it had anything to do with the Baal worship scandal, as the woman is a Midianite, not a Moabite. Remember, Moses himself had married a Midianite, Zipporah, so what's wrong with them doing that? Their deaths were an atonement that succeeded in stemming the plague. What plague? Hadn't the crucifixion already averted the wrath of Yahweh?

> And Israel abode in Shittim; and the people began to play the harlot with the daughters of Moab: for they called the people unto the sacrifices of their gods; and the people did eat, and bowed down to their gods. And Israel joined himself unto Baal-peor: and the anger of Yahweh was kindled against Israel. And Yahweh said unto Moses, Take all the chiefs of the people, and hang them up unto Yahweh before the sun, that the fierce anger of Yahweh may turn away from Israel. And Moses said unto the judges of Israel, Slay ye every one his men that have joined themselves unto Baal-peor.

> And, behold, one of the children of Israel came and brought unto his brethren a Midianitish woman in the sight of Moses, and in the sight of all the congregation of the children of Israel, while they were weeping at the door of the tent of meeting. And when Phinehas, the son of Eleazar, the son of Aaron the priest, saw it, he rose up from the midst of the congregation, and took a spear in his hand; and he went after the man of Israel into the pavilion, and thrust both of them through, the man of Israel, and the woman through her body. So the plague was stayed from the children of Israel. And those that died by the plague were twenty and four thousand.

> And Yahweh spake unto Moses, saying, Phinehas, the son of

Eleazar, the son of Aaron the priest, hath turned my wrath away from the children of Israel, in that he was jealous with my jealousy among them, so that I consumed not the children of Israel in my jealousy. Wherefore say, Behold, I give unto him my covenant of peace: and it shall be unto him, and to his seed after him, the covenant of an everlasting priesthood; because he was jealous for his God, and made atonement for the children of Israel.

Now the name of the man of Israel that was slain, who was slain with the Midianitish woman, was Zimri, the son of Salu, a prince of a fathers' house among the Simeonites. And the name of the Midianitish woman that was slain was Cozbi, the daughter of Zur; he was head of the people of a fathers' house in Midian.

And Yahweh spake unto Moses, saying, Vex the Midianites, and smite them; for they vex you with their wiles, wherewith they have beguiled you in the matter of Peor, and in the matter of Cozbi, the daughter of the prince of Midian, their sister, who was slain on the day of the plague in the matter of Peor. [Numbers 25:1-18, ASV]

One has to suspect that the execution of the mixed couple stems from the same (sort of) milieu that generated the stories of Nehemiah's xenophobia after the Exile. Presumably the plague turned aside by their deaths had been Yahweh's judgment for the Israelite marrying a foreigner, else why would their death have made the difference (just as the death of Achan and his family ended the losing streak occasioned by his sin in snitching a fancy suit from the sacred spoils of war in Josh. 7). The compiler must have seen some similarity between Zimri's crime of being unequally yoked with the heathen Cozbi and the fraternization between Israelites and idolatrous Moabite women, then figured, "Moabites, Midianites—what's the difference?"

Notes

1. Noth, *Exodus: A Commentary*. Trans. J.S. Bowden. Old Testament Library (Philadelphia: Westminster Press, 1962), p. 142.

2. Noth, *History of Pentateuchal Traditions*, p. 166.

3. Noth, *Exodus*, p. 142.

4. Noth, *Exodus*, p. 143.

Conclusion

The Mystery of Moses

Should we speak of Moses' death, or of his departure? Deuteronomy 34:1-8 does use the word "death," that's for sure, but the text is also a bit cagey.

> And Moses went up from the plains of Moab unto mount Nebo, to the top of Pisgah, that is over against Jericho. And Yahweh showed him all the land of Gilead, unto Dan, and all Naphtali, and the land of Ephraim and Manasseh, and all the land of Judah, unto the hinder sea, and the South, and the Plain of the valley of Jericho the city of palm-trees, unto Zoar. And Yahweh said unto him, This is the land which I sware unto Abraham, unto Isaac, and unto Jacob, saying, I will give it unto thy seed: I have caused thee to see it with thine eyes, but thou shalt not go over thither. So Moses the servant of Yahweh died there in the land of Moab, according to the word of Yahweh. And he buried him in the valley in the land of Moab over against Beth-peor: but no man knoweth of his sepulchre unto this day. And Moses was a hundred and twenty years old when he died: his eye was not dim, nor his natural force abated. And the children of Israel wept for Moses in the plains of Moab thirty days: so the days of weeping in the mourning for Moses were ended. [Deut. 34:1-8, ASV]

There is a strange similarity between this story and that of the temptation of Jesus by the devil in Matthew 4:8-9: "The devil took him to a very high mountain and showed him all the kingdoms of the world and the glory of them; and he said to him, 'All these I will give you if you will fall down and worship me.'" It is also found in Luke 4:5-7 and is thus regarded as a Q passage.

However, Marcion's Ur-Lukas did not contain this story. So I am inclined to think Marcionites were correct in charging that Catholic redactors added what the Ur-Lukas lacked.[1] Hence I believe Matthew expanded Mark's brief temptation story (Mark 1:12-13), adapting material from Deuteronomy, depicting Jesus recapitulating Israel's wilderness trials but succeeding where they failed. He has Jesus explicitly cite the appropriate Deuteronomy texts (Deut. 8:3 in Matt. 4:4; Deut. 6:16 in Matt. 4:7; Deut. 6:13 in Matt. 4:10). Perhaps it makes sense to suggest that Matthew adapted the scene of Yahweh taking Moses to a mountain peak to show him the outspread lands that Israel would one day rule.

But the surprising feature of Deuteronomy's Moses obituary is the statement that his burial place remained unknown and unvenerated. How could that be? One might suggest that the location of his grave was kept secret for fear that people would worship Moses. But as the sheer fact of the grave would attest Moses' mortality, it seems unlikely. The inference of the ancients was that there was no grave because there was no corpse. Moses had not really died but, like Enoch and Elijah, was assumed bodily into heaven. Josephus relates Moses' ascension.

> And as he was going to embrace Eleazar and Joshua, and was still discoursing with them, a cloud stood over him on the sudden, and he disappeared in a certain valley, although he wrote in the holy books that he died, which was done out of fear, lest they should venture to say, that because of his extraordinary virtue, he went to God.[2]

Josephus seems to be winking at the reader, implying that Moses had written of his death and burial because he was afraid for them to know what was actually going to happen. In Philo's *Life of Moses*, the law-giver gets "buried," but it is a peculiar burial—up, not down, and by angels who therefore "entombed" him in heaven.

> When he was now on the point of being taken away, and was standing at the very starting-place, as it were, that he might fly away and complete his journey to heaven, he was once more inspired and filled with the Spirit, and while still alive, he prophesied admirably, what should happen to himself after his death, how he had died when he was not as yet dead, and how he was buried without anyone being present so as to know of his tomb, because in fact he was entombed not by mortal hands, but by immortal powers, so that he was not placed in the tomb of his forefathers, having met with particular grace that no man ever saw.[3]

Jude verse 9 alludes to the lost text *The Assumption of Moses*, referring to an argument between the archangel Michael and his opposite number, the devil, over who had the right to Moses' corpse. Each had a case to make. Satan must have argued that the same peccadillo that kept Moses out of the Promised Land ought to bar him from heaven as well. Michael must have countered that Moses had discharged his debt by his exclusion from Canaan and now was clear to join Yahweh in heaven.

The gospel Transfiguration narrative has Moses accompany Elijah to meet Jesus on the mountain top, implying that he was available for the job, having gone alive into heaven as Elijah did. Likewise, he joins Elijah in Revelation chapter 11, engaged in his old pursuit of inflicting plagues on the sinners.

All this hints strongly of the survival of the memory of who and what Moses must originally have been: a sun god. Consider the parallel to Psalm 19:4c-8:

In [the heavens] he has set a tent for the sun,
   Which comes forth like a bridegroom leaving his chamber,
   And, like a strong man, runs its course with joy.
   Its rising is from the end of the heavens,
   And its circuit to the [other] end of them;
   And there is nothing hid from its heat.
   The law of [Yahweh] is perfect,
      Reviving the soul;
   The testimony of [Yahweh] is sure,
      Making wise the simple;
   The precepts of [Yahweh] are right,
      Rejoicing the heart;
   The commandment of [Yahweh] is pure,
      enlightening the eyes.[4]

Samson ("the sun") is obviously a sun god, and we can recognize his portrait here, a strong man whom we see at a seven-day wedding feast, hence in his honeymoon bungalow, as in Pss. 19:5. But with Moses the parallels are even clearer. He enters the Tent of Meeting to receive new commandments from Yahweh and emerges with his face radiant like the sun (Exod. 34:29-35). Psalm 19 seems to shift gears suddenly, dropping the sun motif to take up the theme of God's commandments, only there is no shift because the ancients associated the giving of the law with the sun god.

Apollo gave laws to his people. The Babylonian sun god *Shamash* (same name as Samson) is shown on a *bas relief* atop the stone tablet of the Code of Hammurabi bestowing those laws on the king. As we now read it, for obvious reasons, Moses has received the laws from the god Yahweh, but Moses' radiant countenance betrays the fact that originally he was the solar source of them and gave them to some mortal king.

And then there's the ascension motif itself: It is a cardinal feature of the sun god myth. The sun rises to the zenith of the heavens on a daily basis. The sun god of raw myth becomes the solar hero of legend. Hercules was originally the sun, as witness his poison arrows, i.e., the arrows of sunstroke, as in Psalm 91:5-6:

> $\mathbf{Y}$ou will not fear the terror of the night
>   nor the arrow that flies by day
>   nor the pestilence that stalks in darkness
>   nor the destruction that wastes at noonday. [5]

The mane of the slain Nemean Lion, which he donned, stands for the sun's rays. His twelve labors are the houses of the Zodiac through which Hercules, as the sun, must pass. Samson's long hair represents the sun's beams, too, and when they are shorn, he goes blind and loses his strength, the condition of the sun on a cloudy day. Moreover, he destroys fields of crops with fire, just like the summer sun. Elijah is "a hairy man," denoting the sun's rays. He calls down fire from heaven to consume his foes, and when his time on earth is done, he, too, rises into the sky, this time, aboard Apollo's flaming sun chariot. Enoch lived three hundred sixty-five years, reflecting the solar calendar. He ascended into the sky where he walked, alongside God, across the heavens every day.

———

So Moses is a figure of myth and legend. That ought to be obvious enough by now. But in the very process of demonstrating his legendary character, we have also shown that he is a narrative incarnation of the Torah itself.

The stories about Moses are stories *about the Torah*, just as the various Jesus stories in the gospels make little sense as bits of a biography of Jesus but very great sense as vehicles for early Christian teachings. Form criticism explains why these fictions exist, why people formulated them and passed them on.

We must, therefore, take Moses seriously as we take the Torah, for Moses *is* the Torah. Nothing more, and nothing less.

Notes

1. John Knox, *Marcion and the New Testament: An Essay in the Early History of the Canon* (Chicago: University of Chicago Press, 1942).

2. *Antiquities of the Jews* IV.VIII. 48, in *Works of Josephus*, p. 123.

3. *Life of Moses* 291, in *The Works of Philo*. Trans. C.D. Yonge (Peabody: Hendrickson Publishers, 1993), p. 517.

4. The RSV's usage of "the LORD" has been changed to "Yahweh" in this quotation.

5. This makes a reference, concealed in translation, to *Namtar*, the sunstroke demon.

Appendix One

Philip R. Davies's Comments

I guess your work on Moses is for a lay readership, since most scholars are probably now reconciled to the idea that Moses did not exist or that if he did we can't distinguish fact from legend. But of course, like most results of critical scholarship, it has not reached the general public and the media do not want to know this sort of thing!

Your work is so far-ranging and touches on so many controversial issues that any detailed comment would need to be as long as your own text! But a few observations might help:

The theory of a compilation of four sources (JEDP) is probably now a minority view; at any rate the latest direction in Pentateuch research is to broadly follow Rendtorff's direction (the logic already anticipated in Noth's great study) of a sequence of themes. As I understand it, the current tendency is to consider the five books as more or less coherent compositions with their own aims and themes, with Numbers being the latest, but possibly much of Genesis is also late. Deuteronomy still seems to the majority anchored in the 7th century, but many of us now regard that as impossible.

Later on, in speaking of the "amphyctyony" you may like to update that in the light of Lemche's dismantling of that idea and the current theory that Israel and Judah were separate entities from the outset and did not form a single society or state, except insofar as the land of Judah under its chiefs was vassal to Israel or to Damascus (or to first one, then the other) before being recognised as a kingdom by the Assyrians in the mid-8th century not long before Israel disappeared as a kingdom.

But at any rate none of this makes the figure of Moses any clearer. It does seem that the Deuteronomistic writing and Chronicles each understand the "law of Moses" differently: for the former it is Deuteronomy itself, namely social legislation, while for Chronicles it is something more like Leviticus – that is, cultic. My own suspicion is that the name of Moses got attached to Deuteronomy at a rather late stage and that generally D-type writing has co-opted Moses as the archetypal prophet figure. Hence Moses *may* be more originally a figure of the cultic traditions. But who knows? For here, too, he may have displaced Aaron to a large degree (you discuss this as well, of course). I really don't envy anyone the task of explaining the enormous intricacies and uncertainties to the layperson!

On the rabbinic material I would only add Neusner's suggestion that *Avot* is a supplement to the Mishnah and rather later than its substantial redaction under Yehudah ha Nasi (Judah the Prince). But it is only his suggestion!

You might also find interesting the accounts of Moses and the origins of the Jews (*sic*) in Manetho and Hecataeus of Abdera, which suggest that stories about him were not fully canonised even by c. 300 BCE. My guess is that the episodes you deal with are indeed representative of the attempt to give flesh to a still-shadowy figure and do not take us anywhere back into history. John van Seters, *The Life of Moses: The Yahwist as Historian in Exodus-Numbers* (1994) is definitely worth reading from the point of view of legendary biography, and since he dates J to the post-monarchic period he may not be too far out in his dating.

I admire the scope of your analysis; given all the uncertainties I can't endorse much of it, but neither can I disprove it! The possibility of Greek cultural influence is certainly more plausible now in the scholarly world than a decade or two ago, and definitely worth examining.

I think I should end with my own favourite theory that Yahweh was a moon god. I don't know whether "mooning" is an idiom equally familiar in the USA, but here it refers to the habit of wearing pants so loosely that when one bends over, the upper part of the buttocks is revealed, resembling, I suppose, a half-moon. Anyway, with Exodus 33:22-23 in mind, I propose Yahweh was a mooning god.

So, in brief: I am not sure what scholars will make of your various suggestions. But since they disagree with each other so much, this is not much to the point. Personally, I find most of it interesting and quite a bit of it plausible. I can imagine that the non-specialist will be either horrified or deeply curious!

—Professor Philip R. Davies,
University of Sheffield

Appendix Two

Thomas L. Thompson: Robert Price's Essay on Moses

Your opening reference to "minimalism" is very unclear: "more radical" than what? I don't know that there is any such claim that the latest (most boring?) kings of Israel and Judah are "legendary figments"! Pekah? Hoshea? Jehoiachim? Zedekiah? There is no such argument in any of the works you cite. The historicity of the biblical narratives in Kings, Chronicles and Jeremiah, on the other hand, is questioned in these studies. In footnote 9, my *Early History of the Israelite People* from 1992 is the better work to cite.

What this has to do with the historicity of the Moses narratives, on the other hand, is a great puzzle—and after reading the entire essay, I fail to understand why you classify the Moses of the Pentateuch as a "legal fiction." Is there a shadow here from the Nuzi tablets or Mendenhall's linking the Moses story to Hittite treaties???

By the time that Garbini, Lemche, Brettler, Davies and I engaged ourselves in writing the books you cite, the debate about the historicity of the Moses narratives was largely over, with only Kitchen and a few of the fundamentalists still holding to some form of historical Moses. A good summation of this early "minimalism" can be found in G.W. Ramsey's *The Quest for the Historical Israel: Reconstructing Israel's Early History* (Atlanta, 1981). In retrospect, I do think it fair to say that nothing of significance regarding the historicity of these tales has appeared since. The most important literature is fairly well known: including, T. L. Thompson, *Historicity of the Patriarchal Narratives* (Berlin: de Gruyter, 1974; reprinted: T&T Clark, 2002; 2014); J. Van Seters, *Abraham in History and Tradition* (New Haven: Yale U, 1975); J. H. Hayes and J. M. Miller, *Israelite and Judean History* (Philadelphia: Westminster, 1977); esp. T. L. Thompson and D. Irvin, "The Joseph and Moses Narratives", *ibidem*, 149-212; D. Irvin, *Mytharion*, AOAT 32 (Neukirchen 1978); T. L. Thompson, "A New Attempt to Date the Patriarchs," JAOS 98 (1978), 76-84; T. L. Thompson, "History and Tradition: A Response to J. B. Geyer," JSOT 15 (1980), 57-61. Since Ramsey's summation of 1981, the historicity of the Moses tradition was passé, apart from fundamentalist circles.

The issues surrounding genre and interpretation, however, were quite engaged and, as you can see especially in Irvin's study, but also in my critique of Van Seters and Geyer, we had moved considerably beyond Gunkel's form critical "historical-critical" adaptation of folklore studies to engage formalism directly. (See, here, my "The Conflict Themes in the Jacob Narratives," *Semeia* 15, 1979, 5-26; *The Origin Tradition of Ancient Israel*, Sheffield: SAP, 1987; "Text, Context and Referent in Israelite Historiography,' in T. L. Thompson, *Biblical Narrative and Palestine's History*, (London: Acumen, 2013), 71-92; "The Intellectual Matrix of Early Biblical Monotheism," *idem*, 105-118; "How Yahweh Became God: Exodus 3 and 6 and the Heart of the Pentateuch," *idem*, 119-132; "4QTestimonia and Bible Competition: A Copenhagen Lego-Hypothesis," *idem*, 133-146; "Why Talk About the Past: The Bible, Epic and Historiography," *idem*, 147-162; "Historiography in the Pentateuch: Twenty-Five Years after Historicity," *idem, 163-182;* "The Messiah Epithet in the Hebrew Bible," *idem, 183-204;* "Kingship and the Wrath of God: or Teaching Humility," *idem*, 205-234; *idem*, "From the Mouth of Babes: Strength: Psalm 8 and the Book of Isaiah," *idem*, 235-250; "Job 29: Biography or Parable?"*idem*, 251-270; "Mesha and Questions of Historicity," *idem*, 271-290; "Imago Dei: a Problem in the Discourse of the Pentateuch," *idem*, 291-304.)

See also my *Messiah Myth: The Near Eastern Roots of Jesus and David* (New York: Basic, 2005); also: "Some Exegetical and Theological Implications of Understanding Exodus as a Collected Tradition," in Lemche and Müller, *Fra dybet: Festskrift til John Strange* (Copenhagen: Museum Tusculanum, 1994) 1-19; "He is Yahweh: He does what is right in his own eyes" in Fatum and Müller, *Tro og Historie: Festskrift til Nils Hyldahl* (Copenhagen: Museum Tysculanum, 1996), 112-128; "Creating the Past: Biblical Narrative as Interpretive Discourse," *Collegium Biblicum Årsskrift*, 1998, 101-119; "A Testimony of the Good King: Reading the Mesha Stele," in L. L. Grabbe, *Ahab Agonistes:The Rise and Fall of the Omride Dynasty* 2007, 236-292 "Mesha and Questions of Historicity;" SJOT 2007, 241-260).

When dealing with the changes of the last fifty years which have been associated with so-called "minimalism," issues of historicity have merely been the most vocal because of the fundamentalist drift in American biblical studies. However, the real issues have been European ones—as can be seen already in John van Seters' dissertation *The Hyksos* and articles of the 1960s (cf. "A Date for the Admonitions in the Second Intermediate Period" in J. Van Seters, *Changing Perspectives 1: Studies in the History, Literature and Religion of Biblical Israel*, Equinox: 2011, 17-30 as well as in Lemche's critique of Noth's amphictyony hypothesis: e.g., "The Greek Amphictyony: Could it Be a Prototype for Israelite Society in the Period of the Judges?" In *Biblical Studies and the Failure of History: Changing Perspectives 3, Acumen: 2013*, 61-68—a thoroughgoing revolt against the dominance of the historical criticism from Wellhausen and Gunkel to Noth and Von Rad.)

In international scholarship today, I don't see that your readings, oriented towards problems that are current in scholarship (and they are not accompanied with a discussion of either method or goals—other than the story's lack of historicity), would arouse much interest. It is a very passive essay and I don't really understand what you want to do with it.

—Thomas L. Thompson,
Professor of Theology at
the University of Copenhagen,
1993–2009

24096677R00074

Printed in Great Britain
by Amazon